**THE TRUTH IS ALLOWED
BUT A BRIEF GLORY
BETWEEN ECCENTRICITY
AND PASSE'**

Unknown

THINK

THINK

OBSERVATIONS ON LIFE
BY A GENERALIST

A HANDBOOK ON UNDERSTANDING

RODNEY CHOATE

Edited by the Author

Front And Back Cover Designs By The Author

FOR THOSE WHO STRUGGLE TO
LIVE THE PRIMARY VIRTUES,
AND THOSE WHO ARE MISUNDERSTOOD
AND MALIGNED FOR IT

CONTENTS

FORWARD

I begin writing in the Spring of the year 2020. Western culture, as we have experienced it, and that of the United States in particular, is nearing its end. It has been a short or long time coming depending on one's perspective. Little sooner had Shallus' ink dried than men began to subvert the U.S. Constitution. A few men sincerely, yet erroneously, believed that if the Document were interpreted too strictly the national government might be "interpreted away". But the motives of the majority of those who did openly take exception to the Constitution were not so honorable. Some men believed that the Document itself – ink on a piece of paper - as well as their old traditions and habits, would be enough to protect them regardless of their own intellectual capacities or behavior. But the honeymoon with the Constitution (what little there was of one) was so short lived that I fear even some of the Founders may have died with broken hearts. Also, people believed that each successive generation would carry on, somehow magically acquiring the necessary qualities of character with little intellectual effort on their own (the elders) part. In other words, everyone "passed the buck". Whether any individual ever realizes it or not, the society will now find out how fragile and precious and probably irreplaceable their modicum of freedom was. Those who have been thinking that, upon some collapse, freedom could be re-established by some kind of armed resistance are in for a rude surprise. Whatever their more remote past, recent past and present Americans are not a very philosophical lot. When the collapse comes most people will not understand what happened nor how it could have been avoided. I have been thinking about life for much of my life and am old enough to have lived through some experiences. I have some novel observations about the human condition that I feel compelled to share.

THE ACT OF EXPLANATION CLARIFIES AN IDEA
NOT ONLY FOR THE RECEIVER BUT
THE SENDER AS WELL.

The Human Side Of Science
Arthur Wiggins / Charles Wynn, Sr.

What are three main goals I hope to accomplish with this Volume? Firstly, in my readings on philosophy there seemed to be quite modest attention given to the **psychological** aspect of things. There is nothing wrong with that. It is wholly appropriate to discuss hard philosophy from a theoretical perspective, giving minimal attention to how individual men might respond to the ideas. Nevertheless, as I thought more about the matter I wondered if it might be possible to integrate some psychology into a basic account of philosophy, thereby creating an interesting and informative read. In due course I came up with some ideas on how that might be done and this Volume is my attempt at that. Secondly, and closely related to the previous goal, I thought that the materials I were reading gave too little guidance on **personal relationships,** leaving too much "wiggle room" for reckless interpretation – and some reckless interpretation did I see! In other words, the revolutionary philosophies I were reading were failing to "revolutionize" personal relationships. So this Volume contains my attempt to fill that perceived gap. And lastly, an always worthy goal is the attempt to **ever simplify the complex** down to greater and greater elegance. I wholeheartedly agree with Oliver Wendell Holmes, Jr., when he said that, "I would not give a fig for simplicity this side of complexity, but would give my life for simplicity on the **other side** of complexity." So this short book is my attempt at a simplification while keeping mindful of the complexities of a more robust philosophical treatise. It is my hope that readers will find these ideas interesting and helpful.

A literature review of writings on man's mental life shows that the field is dominated by a mechanical as opposed to a volitional view of it. Indeed, all popular viewpoints seem aloof on the effect of volition on the human condition. As Joseph Weizenbaum lamented in his 1976 book, Computer Power and Human Reason: "What is it about the computer that has brought the view of man as a machine to a new level of plausibility?". That thinking people of today are not even more alarmed than Weizenbaum in 1976, is distressing. In a scan of Wikipedia articles such as "Cognitive Psychology", "Cognitive Therapy", "Psychology Of Reasoning", and "Concept Learning", I saw no explicit reference to, let alone discussion of, human volition or free will. The Wiki article on "Volition" itself was rather short, while the article on "Free Will" was more

F-2

extensive, but, in my opinion, neither are as helpful as what I shall be describing in this Volume! It remains a mystery to me why Wiki maintains **separate** articles on "Volition" and "Free Will". Why? Are they not the same thing?!

When questioned, a clear majority of people across all disciplines claim to believe in "free will". The problem is that many do not seem to practice this belief. A 2014, special edition of National Geographic Magazine -Your Personality: Explained, claims that "about 50% of variation in personality can be attributed to our genes". The remainder of personality was then attributed to "the environment"-- yet it was then acknowledged (apparently oblivious to the obvious self-contradiction) that "parenting and household environment" were **unable** to be pinpointed by researchers as a major impact on personality. Are not our formative childhood growing conditions our major environmental influence?!! There was no discussion whatever regarding volition on the formation of our personalities.

This silence regarding volition comes from either taking it for granted (a bad idea), or minimizing or denying it (a false idea). To be charitable, this attitude may be due, at least in small part, to a misunderstanding of volition and this Book was written to fully address that problem. So crucial and central to this Book is the issue, I should take a few moments to give examples of how this insidious mechanistic attitude towards man expresses itself, so that you might understand:

    a)   **"Democracy will save us"** - There are those who believe that the mere conglomerate of opinions and actions of people can preserve civilization; as if a mob somehow had some innate intelligence un-possessed by individuals. (Many individuals exhibiting this belief are not being honest. Remember this point when reading the bottom of page 32.)

    b)   **"Information will save us"** – There are those who believe that the mere free access and flow of information and knowledge can somehow preserve civilization.

    c)   **"Education will save us"** – There are those who believe that simply farming the young out to schools (as they are currently constituted) would be enough to preserve civilization.

d) **"Freedom of speech, press, etc. will save us"** – There are those who believed that the simple possession of our freedoms would have been enough to preserve civilization.

e) **"Technology will save us"** – There are those who believe that the simple march of science and technology was all that man needed.

f) **"Government programs will save us"** – There are those who believe that the state can centrally plan prosperity for the people. (Ditto when reading the bottom of page 32.)

g) **"Protection of minorities will save us"** – There are those who believe that the identification and protection of special groups of people play any role in preserving civilization.

h) **"A vibrant, successful economy will save us"** – There are those who believe that ever-greater economic success of the individual and/or society will preserve civilization.

i) **"Communication will save us"** – There are those who believe that the mere free flow of ideas and knowledge **between** individuals will preserve civilization.

j) **"Historical Cycles"** – There are those who believe that societies are inevitably pre-destined to go through cycles of rise-and-fall, good times and bad.

k) **"Advertising, media, movies, are the cause of materialism, violence, etc."** - There are those who believe that man simply absorbs his ideas and principles like a sponge.

All of the above measures and conditions have existed or been tried, and all have failed. All assume a mechanistic view of man where he can achieve the right "output" if only he receives the right "input".

The mechanistic, non-volitional view of man is largely played out on the battlefield of the "Nature vs. Nurture" argument, (as seen above). Both viewpoints do have certain facts to commend them, and both represent a mechanistic view of man – the one of man as a "living stone" expressing his innate behaviors; the other of man as a billiard ball pushed about by his environment. Both extremes deny, or ignore, the "third rail" of volition in man. These attitudes are seized upon by the snake oil salesmen of society as they speak of chronically troubled masses of people as if their personal psychology play little role in their continued troubles, and that their salvation lies in little more than a massive influx of material goods provided by others. This mechanistic non-volitional view of man dominates virtually all thought and discussion of man and his problems. Human individuality is indeed touted by society, but only as the result of varying "innate tendencies" or environmental influences. Some thinkers, such as the late E.O. Wilson, for example, hold that man is torn between a genetically determined "good" group-think nature, and a (somehow acquired) "bad" individualistic nature. This Book is a marked departure from all these points of view, and was written in the hope of explaining the human condition in a way that the reader might find more fruitful.

It is not my intention to "reinvent wheels" in writing this Book, nor to repeat good work already done by others. As such, this Book is built on an **existing philosophical framework.** My goal is to provide some observations of mine with enough background in philosophy that the reader might hold my thoughts in their proper perspective to the whole. So this need not be a particularly big book. It is my hope that a shorter book might be read by more people. It is also not my intention to present specialized knowledge possessed only by professionals in any field – my claim is that the observations herein are for "everyman".

> IF I HAVE SEEN FURTHER IT IS BY STANDING
> ON THE SHOULDERS OF GIANTS.
> Isaac Newton

I am indebted to a great many thinkers whom I have encountered in my life. As such, at the end of the Book I have included a rather extensive list of resource material. So, one purpose of including such a list is to give credit to those who have come before me, and from whom I have learned. To any of my teachers that I have inadvertently omitted, I am sorry. Secondly, the reader is greatly encouraged to consider all this material, and in particular that dealing with more extensive treatments of philosophy. I have, with understandable reluctance, pared the list down somewhat to those works that I felt the most important. Don't be surprised that the resource material is quite varied -- that is important as you should understand in due course. The list is to be considered an integral part of this Book – which, again, you should understand as you read. The reference to any thinker in this Volume should not be construed to mean that I agree with all of their conclusions or behaviors. And lastly, it is important that a good book point to other good books. The rational man is a faithful reader and greatly values this in his books.

THE PROBLEM IS NOT THAT (PEOPLE) ARE SPECIALIZING,
BUT THAT SPECIALISTS ARE GENERALIZING.
Viktor Frankl
Psychiatrist, Holocaust Survivor

FEYNMAN QUIETLY NURSED A SOLUTION SO
RADICAL AND STRAIGHTFORWARD THAT IT
COULD HAVE APPEALED ONLY TO SOMEONE
IGNORANT OF THE (existing) LITERATURE.
GENIUS: The Life And Science
Of Richard Feynman
James Gleick

Who am I to write these Parts? After all, I'm no expert. Why should you put any trust in what I have to say? We are living in a time when truth and frankness, hard to come by in any age, have become almost nonexistent in mainstream public discourse. Politicians, media concerns, and the "experts" are lying to the public – **leaving the person of average insight helpless.** "Bad money", as well as the publics' desire for false and easy solutions, has corrupted the system, I fear, past the point of no return. It has been said that an "expert" is someone who knows more and more about less and less until he knows everything about nothing. It turns out that one particular problem with "experts" is that they usually make their money in life by being experts – otherwise they would not have gone to the trouble of becoming experts. Then, in order to sell their "product" to enough "customers", their own understanding of things had to be held back to the level of interest and integrity of their audience. Generally, they really believe their own construction of the way things are since most regular human beings aren't evil enough to **consciously** think one thing and peddle something else. More broadly, "experts" are usually people just like anybody else, subject to the same virtues and shortcomings I will be discussing in this Book!

Still, you deserve some answer to "who am I to write to you?" I was born in 1958, shortly before Mother's Day, in Abbeville, in south Louisiana, amid the local rice farming. I spent warm summer nights going to sleep by the bull frogs. The hospital in which I was born was a large wood-frame building called The Palms, in Vermilion Parish (or "County"). Where the hospital once stood is now the Parish library. Prior to entering their schooling neither of my parents spoke English but rather the local French dialect. At one point my paternal grandfather was literally a trapper, somewhere around the turn of the century (1900), while my maternal grandfather was said, by my mother, to have been the first welder in town. I never met my grandmothers as they died fairly young and I was born

F-6

when my father was 40 years old. I grew up a country boy, three miles outside of town. According to personality testing I was supposed to become some kind of teacher or counselor by the figuring of those people. So of course I became an engineer by training and read all kinds of books during my life to make up for that "mistake". At their best, engineers study things to figure out how they work. I bring an uncommon logic, and I hope honesty, to this particular subject and I have some fresh observations about life that I think the reader may not have considered before. The world is a screwed up place, **when compared to the way things could be**, because so many things are done that are just not right. There will be no salvation from the "top-down" – the people in charge are too corrupted. If the people in charge are to ever start doing things right they are going to need some other people around **who will be expecting it of them!** I would also like to help any person who happens by my book. That is partly why I write.

I'm not asking that the reader take anything in this Book on faith, for that would be a mistake. I would like you to think for yourself. What if I'm all wrong in my observations, or even wrong in the single smallest detail? What about any information or details that I have left out of this work, either by accident, laziness, or necessity? What about all the crooks and charlatans producing confusing and misleading materials? What will you do then? Just think for yourself. I want you to discover my errors and see what is NOT in here for whatever reason. The world needs more, many more, people who are dedicated to good thinking and rooting out errors rather than simply being spoon fed their ideas. That is how real progress will be made. My most optimistic hope is that many years from now the reader will find that some of my observations in this work have stood the test of time, and a fair hearing.

THE BEST PROBLEM IS THE ONE THAT NEVER HAPPENS.
The Author

THE CHIEF CAUSE OF PROBLEMS IS SOLUTIONS
Eric Sevareid

One of the first points I'd like to present to you is what I call "problem oriented" vs. "solution oriented" thinking. A speaker on CSPAN, some time back, said that "most people know more what they don't like than how to solve the problem." The point was also expressed quite nicely in the 1970 song, "Ride Captain Ride":

F-7

Seventy-three men sailed up from the San Francisco Bay,
Rolled off their ship, and here's what they had to say.
"We're callin' everyone to ride along to another shore;
We can laugh our lives away and be free once more".
But no one heard them callin', no one came at all,
Cause they were too busy watchin' those old raindrops fall.
As a storm was blowin' out on the peaceful sea,
Seventy-three men sailing off to history.

Almost all the discourse one hears regarding problems just amounts to bitching about problems and proposing "solutions" that only create **more problems!** The psychology involved amounts to -- "The problem is that we have this problem, and so our problem is we have to get rid of this problem."; or "Look at all the terrible things that people have done in the past. We must 'never forget', in order to prevent such things from happening again." However, as you read this Book it should become clear to you why even many millions of men, knowing very well the mistakes of men in the past, will do **nothing** to prevent the same evils from being committed in the future!

In a book I'm now reading, a black, inner-city policeman asked the journalist, "How come these political scientists did not foresee the social problems in the cities and have plans in place to avoid them?". The journalist had no answer for the man, but I do. The problems were caused, first, by a century of white peoples' failure to enforce equal rights, and then decades of attempts to address the results of that with welfare! (An Empire Wilderness, Robert D. Kaplan)

Problem oriented thinking is a manifestation of **pragmatism**. Pragmatism holds that the comprehension an independent reality is not a purpose of thinking -- i.e., problems are "fluid" and we must always be "flexible". One motto of the pragmatist is: "the worst thing we can do is nothing." (We contrast "pragmatism" with the **practical man,** who observes the actual results of his policies and adjusts his opinions accordingly. Learning by trial-and-error is certainly better than not learning at all.) Problem oriented thinking is **reactionary.** The problem oriented thinker doesn't understand what he did to contribute to his own catastrophes. Today, in my town, one high school boy killed another, with a gun. There seem to be an abnormal number of killings lately. A teary-eyed teacher from the school said, "I wish I knew how to stop these things, I feel so helpless." What the teacher really meant was – "how can this violence stop **without me changing myself in any way?"** To give another subtle example of problem oriented thinking: there is a notion out there (mostly among non-professionals I hope) that only someone who has had your problem can best help you with your problem. However, quite to the contrary, if you have a problem shouldn't you feel more confident talking with someone who knows how to have never had that problem? Notice again the subtle complaint: "how can I be helped without changing myself?" The fact is that there are few people around who understand why they have never had some particular problem, so sometimes you are just stuck with someone who has previously "handled" your problem. Someone once said that for every 999 people hacking at the branches of evil, only one is hacking at the roots. People are intelligent and clever creatures and **would solve the world's man-made problems if they wanted to solve them.** The reason why the World's man-made problems never get solved is because the great solutions needed to solve them, **1)** conflict with people's existing belief systems and the things that people think that others owe them, and **2)** some trouble and effort are required to scrap and re-build significant portions of one's world view.

So one purpose of these Parts is to call attention to the reasons that people don't solve problems and actively create problems in the world. A real solution to a problem may at first sight appear to be some distance from the problem itself. This is because a real solution is **a way of being and living** which prevents the problem from recurring or even having happened in the first place! I wish to create the **intention** in the reader to solve problems and show the thinking needed to solve them! I wish to show the reader that right thinking and living are consistent with **one's own self-interest.**

> THE SLENDEREST OF KNOWLEDGE THAT MAY BE OBTAINED
> OF THE HIGHEST THINGS IS MORE DESIRABLE THAN THE
> MOST CERTAIN KNOWLEDGE THAT MAY BE OBTAINED
> OF THE LESSER THINGS.
> Saint Thomas Aquinas

It will be a challenge for me to describe some forthcoming ideas to the reader, and perhaps difficult for the reader to apprehend them. This is **not** because the ideas will be particularly complex, but rather because of their **simple unfamiliarity.** I will be discussing in what are called **"concepts"** and most people are not used to this. Remember, I'm not an "expert" just re-packaging what you already know in order to sell it back to you. For all our intelligence, most people are not used to thinking about new things in new ways. Other than what people do in their jobs to earn money, and their hobbies, many people gain very little useful knowledge after their teen years. So the mind gets used to running through its days on a kind of automatic pilot that I call **"thinking in clichés".** Any discourse must be about existing understanding presented in the form of the appropriate clichés, otherwise the listener's eyes glass over, his hair hurts, etc., and the conversation is over. Occasionally an "expert" re-packages the old wisdom into new clichés, (or at least some clichés that haven't been used in a while), writes a book, gets rich, and off the society goes on its latest "self-help" craze. And the more things change, the more they stay the same. So pay attention because there are some novel observations I want to share with you. In some cases a paragraph, or even a single sentence, will hit the reader up with multiple unfamiliar ideas that are going to confuse. Not only that, but the unfamiliar ideas might only be able to be understood **when considered together!** I have made every effort to make the material as fluid and readable as I could. One good strategy to help cope with the simple unfamiliarity of thinking in concepts, if one feels bogged down, is to go back and read a section, or Part, over.

> He felt embarrassed to have spent so much time on a calculation
> that now seemed trivial and self-evident. As far as he knew, it
> was useless. He had never seen a reference to it by another
> scientist. So he was surprised to hear, in 1948, that a controversy
> had erupted among physical chemists about the discovery, now
> known as the Feynman Theorem, or the Feynman-Hellmann Theorem.
> Some scientists felt it was too simple to be true.
> GENIUS: The Life And Science
> Of Richard Feynman
> James Gleick

> HOW EXTREMELY STUPID (of us)
> NOT TO HAVE THOUGHT OF THAT.
> Thomas Huxley on Charles Darwin

That being said, don't think that what I have to say about life is complicated. A seemingly complicated problem is nothing but a number of simple problems rolled into one. In fact, once I start writing stuff you are going to think how ridiculously simple it is. The real difficulty is in understanding **idea systems** and putting them into practice. There will be much remaining work to be done. A big problem is that after people have read something they think they automatically know something. What is needed by people is the right foundation, which I hope to show. No real knowledge gained by you in the future will contradict anything I have to say in this Book. I am merely going to break complex knowledge down into its constituent parts so it can be dealt with.

> "NO THINKING OR FEELING PERSON CAN DENY EITHER NATURE'S GRANDEUR
> OR THE DEPTH AND DIGNITY OF OUR DISCOVERY..........."
> Stephen J. Gould
> Essay: "A Division Of Worms"
> NATURAL HISTORY

Nor will I be destroying the mystery or excitement of life by attempting to explain it. This is a terrible, destructive fear that people have – that life will become boring once problems are solved, or certain things that **can** be understood, **become** understood. "Mystery" is the concept referring to the things in life that cannot be known by any man. The refusal to know important things that can be known is called "stupidity". There is more mystery and excitement in the way things really are than in all the lies you have been told by the fearful, lazy and corrupt people in your life. David Dietz in his 1931 book, The Story Of Science:

> The ancient Psalmist in Biblical days felt the glory of the heavens. One imagines him standing in the open fields at night, filled with awe at the wonder and grandeur off the star-filled firmament. And yet his conception of the heavens was a simple one compared with what modern astronomy has revealed about them. If the sight of the stars filled him with awe, then we ought to feel his wonder a thousand times over, knowing what modern astronomy has to tell.

Or Richard Feynman:

> I (a scientist) too can see the stars on a desert night, and feel them. But do I see less, or more?........ It does no harm to the mystery to know a little about it. Far more marvelous is the truth than any artists of the past imagined it...... What kind of men are poets who can speak of Jupiter if he is a Greek God, but if he is a great mass of spinning methane and ammonia must remain silent?
>
> Richard Feynman
> The Pleasure Of Finding Things Out

Or, to put the matter another way: Why, if in order to be considered good, must an idea **play only to its audiences' ignorance?** In fact, paradoxically, it is the un-knowing man who cannot tolerate ambiguity, uncertainty, mystery. Looked at honestly, it is the un-knowing man who feels he must understand everything by explaining the unexplainable; he feels he must "up-stage" the knowing man. Philip Wylie:

> **Disillusionment** seems painful to most men because they live by **illusion**,,,,,,to any man who searches for truth, his most welcome and desired experience is disillusionment. For when he achieves it he knows he has erased one error and set up a better image, or a way to one,,,,,,,,But that most glorious experience is not ardently sought. Illusion,,,,as the basis of man's usual image means that to be **un-deceived** in any one way, however small, threatens the sum of all delusions. (emphasis mine)
>
> Philip Wylie
> The Magic Animal

So, in fact, understanding life is not an impediment to mystery and wonder, but a **requirement for it --** but I'm getting ahead of myself.

Before proceeding further in this work you should agree on a number of stipulations. First, any agreements or disagreements you might have with these ideas should be fact based, reality based. There should be some thing or fact that one can point to, to say, "yes, this observation agrees (or disagrees) with the position put forth". I understand that the burden of proof is on "he who asserts the positive", and I will certainly be making assertions in this work and not be doing rigorous proofs in every case. But this is not a particularly scholarly work and one is not being asked to just believe anything written here. What I'm asking is that you try these ideas out and see for yourself if they are true.

The next stipulation is that a philosophy is not to be built on what are called "life boat" situations. So you must not point to some kind of strange or emergency situation to disprove these ideas. Lifeboat situations are those that render man's power of choice useless, while this Book is about those things that are open to man's choice. True "life boat" situations are rare and negate the power of choice. As long as men have meaningful options there is no, so called, "life boat" situation.

A related stipulation is that these ideas only hold true for man in a free society. Living in an unfree society places man in the "life boat" situation mentioned previously, where man's power of reason is rendered useless in meeting his needs. Living in an unfree society is a kind of cancer which eats away and eventually destroys individuals and the social fabric. So to the extent that one is not in a free society then these ideas might not strictly apply.

> HE WHO KNOWS ONLY HIS OWN SIDE OF THE CASE
> KNOWS LITTLE OF THAT.
> John Stuart Mill

> THERE'S A TIME TO SEEK OPPOSING VIEWS,
> AND A TIME TO DECIDE ONE HAS HEARD ENOUGH.
> David Kelley

This Volume is quite the opposite of a "how to book". At first I considered organizing this work into "Part 1, Theory" and "Part 2, Practice" sections, but elected not to for the following reasons. If I did include a "practice" part it would not be in the spirit of making the reader wrong for disagreeing with my conclusions, but rather to teach; to illustrate the process of reasoning one's way to correct conclusions. But therein lies the crux of a problem which this Book is intended to address. Most people are quite "subjective" in their thinking (though they don't see themselves that way) and don't really believe in objective truth, but rather in "my conclusions" vs. "your conclusions" -- a totally irrational and combative approach to knowledge -- i.e., people are not "objective". Upon having a "clarity of moment" in discussion with such people, their telltale response is, "well, everyone is entitled to his own opinion". In fact, while everyone is indeed entitled to his opinion, it is impossible for everyone to always be right.

The purpose of this Book is to help people **suspend their conclusions and just think!** One must first know how to think! So I'm being honest with you now. I do not know everything, but I know what I know. So, with the possible exception of Part 5, this Book doesn't have as many conclusions or prescriptions as it might. This is something that you, the reader, will have to accomplish. The ideas presented herein are just too important to kill by writing a book that the reader will simply throw away because he doesn't like my conclusions. I realize that this is a very strong point to make. I am sorry but that's just the way things are. I want to show the reader how to think, not argue with anyone. I will try to limit conclusions to those reasonable to show as part of the thinking process. Nevertheless, it is not possible, nor would it be honest, to write a book such as this without a point of view -- so the reader will be left with little doubt as to where I'm coming from. I further elaborate on this issue in Part 5, in the Topic called "Polarization" (page 100)– the term pretty much speaks for itself, I would say. You are welcome to go and read that topic now if you don't mind getting ahead of ourselves, as that might be of some benefit.

I want to remind the reader that even the best rules may have exceptions. We are dealing with people here and not the physical sciences. That's why it's called The Humanities. One may always find cases that might not fit the stated generalizations, but such cases would be less common than one might think. It is only by generalizing that we can know anything. If every problem that man ever faced had to be dealt with afresh, as a child facing anything for the first time, we would have no knowledge. The trick is recognizing quickly whether an existing policy fits a particular situation.

I want to emphasize that your education up to this point has largely been about telling you WHAT to think, but not HOW to think. Everyone in your life up to this point,,,,,,, parents, teachers, etc., have been telling you what to think. Unless one has had a very special teacher along the way, you likely have had no formal instruction on how to think, **and this work will be your very first exposure.** (And we will never know how many marginal or child geniuses are lost along the way for the lack of such instruction.) One reason why you are so hard-headed and unwilling to improve your positions is because you do not know how to think well, although there are other reasons as well. It's as if you are stranded on an ocean shore with a magnificent ship that you do not know how to sail! This Book is about how to sail that ship. There is a correct destination, but no one can just tell you where that is. That is something that each person must decipher independently.

Lastly, I wish to give the reader this point to consider: Our children are the future and we have failed the future. Our methods thus far have been **worse** than a crap shoot. If I ask a man to journey to a place I should not expect him to reach it without a map. This Book is part of that map – the learning to read the map is the learning of the Book. So lets explore the terrain and see what happened.

Rodney Choate

Alexandria, Louisiana

April, 2022

RATS

A Ph.D. of research psychology, at an eastern university, noticed that rats trained to run some test, to receive food, quickly unlearn the behavior when no food is found, while so many people are never able to unlearn their own bad behaviors regardless of the pain and troubles thereby caused. Hoping to help people, the good doctor was determined to discover what quality gave the rats the desirable flexibility and so devised many experiments to study rats and discover the factor (expending much government grant money in the process). After much time, effort and expense the doctor came up empty - there was apparently no special factor which accounted for "rat flexibility".

But the doctor had a good engineer friend, who also had the hobby of thinking about philosophy on the side. One day, over lunch, the doctor explained the problem to his friend. "Of course!" said his friend, "I solved THAT problem some years ago. You've been trying to learn too much about people by studying rats. I study PEOPLE! Your rats unlearn their behaviors when finding no food because there are no other rats around to manipulate or force into giving up their stuff".

The doctor's jaw relaxed slightly and he dropped his fork.

PART 1: FOR THE LOVE OF WISDOM

FOR YEARS I WORKED ON THE PROBLEM OF GRAVITY.
THEN, ONE DAY I HAD THE MOST BEAUTIFUL THOUGHT.
WHEN I USED MY THEORY TO CALCULATE THE ORBIT
OF MERCURY EXACTLY, I COULD NOT FUNCTION FOR DAYS.
Albert Einstein

Philosophy is the process of logically inquiring into the nature of human life with the goal of prescribing the requirements for "the good life". The word "philosophy" comes from Greek terms meaning "love of wisdom". A right philosophy is desperately needed by every person, yet it is scoffed at by the public, and the field of professionals is populated largely by "experts" (see "experts" in the Forward to this Book, page F-6). The result is that most of the human population of life on earth, all BILLIONS of them, behave more like extremely intelligent animals than the rational beings of which they are capable. It is fairly uncommon to find an individual who has largely settled for himself the fundamental issues of life. Most people are, at least to some extent, muddling their way through. Commonly, one finds men who consider themselves good, yet retain flaws in their thinking which are like a cancer that, when combined with the flaws in the thinking of others, create the tragic cycles of hope and despair that history records.

A proper philosophy consists of at least four topics, all of which are important and three of which will need to be discussed in some detail in separate parts – thereby forming the main body of this Book. A good philosophy consists of at least the following areas of inquiry:

1 -   METAPHYSICS (A view on the fundamental nature of existence)
This topic sets a number of important RULES, or BOUNDARIES for our thinking which are needed to help keep our thinking honest and on track.

So, where to begin a philosophy? We begin with what we know. We begin with the fact that our sense organs are gathering information about a universe that we assume exists, and of which we are aware. Asking for further proof of existence or awareness assumes the existence of a creature able to prove it, so such reasoning would be circular. Any philosophy imagined has to start somewhere, so we start with existence itself. So the

1

primary error in philosophy would be to ask for proofs of existence and/or awareness. Logically, and in a similar fashion, the converse of this error would be to dispense with man's awareness of existence and NOT ask for proof of everything else, as if man's awareness didn't matter!

So, what works in metaphysics is well summed up in the phrase "This Is It!". What that means is that there is only one universe that we inhabit, and it is all that affects our lives. The existence of the universe is not to be questioned, it just is! All the information that we can ever know, or need, is received through our senses about the things that exist around us. The universe "makes sense". Nature makes no mistakes --- only man makes mistakes. Any deviation from these rules will lead to grave errors in thinking.

Should the reader disagree with these metaphysical starting points, he must understand just what he is disagreeing with. We are simply starting our thinking with what we KNOW, and will continue on with what we know, or with things for which there is evidence, or at least some plausibility. We have no reason to think otherwise.

2 - EPISTEMOLOGY (A theory on how we think and know things)
This will be discussed in Part 2.

3 - ETHICS (Dealing with issues faced by the individual **NOT** in relation to others) This will be discussed in Part 3.

4 - POLITICS (Dealing with issues faced by the individual **IN** relation to others) This will be discussed in Part 4.

We will now delve more deeply into the last three topics.

THE LORD GOD IS SUBTLE,
BUT MALICIOUS HE IS NOT.
Albert Einstein

GREAT IS PHILOSOPHY,
FOR IT IS THE SYNTHESIS OF ALL KNOWLEDGE.
BUT IF IT IS TO BE TRUE PHILOSOPHY
IT MUST BE BUILT UPON SCIENCE,
WHICH IS TESTED KNOWLEDGE.
Edwin G. Conklin

PART 2: EPISTEMOLOGY
(A THEORY ON HOW WE THINK AND KNOW THINGS)

LET US FIRST UNDERSTAND THE FACTS,
AND THEN WE MAY SEEK THE CAUSE.
Aristotle

The study of epistemology is important for two main reasons. Obviously, it is important for a man to have a theory of how his knowledge is acquired. But there is an important psychological reason as well. A man needs the confidence of knowing **that** he can know. It is likely that the reader has, to a greater or lesser extent, been denied all of this knowledge by the cultures in which we live. Furthermore, and although I'm once again getting ahead of myself, some men are in want of **permission** to think for themselves – and they will never break away, and do so, unless they know **how.** Therefore, it is important to study this Part even though it may seem dry or technical. It is important to have in the background of one's thinking that one has been explained that he can know things, and something of how that process works. In particular, we wish to bring the thinking process **closer to the consciousness** where it can be dealt with **volitionally.** This will soon become more clear.

As previously alluded to, this Part is not intended to be an exhaustive account of how the mind-brain operates. Such a discussion is beyond the scope of my intentions in this Book, nor am I even qualified to write such an account. Even among the "experts" there seems to be at least as much opinion as hard facts regarding the matter. Rather, this Part is intended to focus on the **volitional** aspects of thinking – the things over which a man has some control.

PHILOSOPHY SEEMS TO BE THE SCIENCE OF MAKING SIMPLE THINGS
DIFFICULT TO UNDERSTAND, BUT I CAN CONCEIVE OF A PHILOSOPHY
WHICH IS THE SCIENCE OF MAKING DIFFICULT THINGS EASY TO UNDERSTAND.
Lin Yutang
The Importance Of Living

THINKING IN PRINCIPLES
Before proceeding further I think I must re-emphasize something that the reader can expect. This Book will attempt to **downplay** telling the reader what to think, while **up-playing** the demonstration of the thinking process itself. This

will involve what is called thinking in "principles", or thinking in "terms of concepts", both on my own part, to write, as well as on the reader's part, to learn. Most people are not used to this. Although the human brain is built to think in concepts, and does so automatically, **it does not automatically do it well !** – this must be accomplished volitionally. Left to its own devices the brain will accumulate a hash of shallow, contradictory principles to live by.

To clarify these points, and drive them home, the following discussion is offered: Take the statement "Thou shall not steal." On its face this looks like a fine statement, and it is. However, the statement (taken by itself) is **completely unusable as a principle** in every society on Earth, and ever has been! Why? The answer is simple – men do not, and never have agreed on exactly **when a man is being stolen from!** (It is as if men have been more concerned about their own souls than their victims!) To answer the question "When is a man being stolen from?", requires a chain of reasoning which this Volume shall undertake. So, to be **operative** a "principle" must not only be clear in its statement, but also clear in the meaning of its words themselves.

Hence, the average person is **un-accustomed to clarity.** The goal of this Book is extra-ordinary clarity and depth, which will be a new experience for many readers. As the reading goes by one should get more comfortable with the flow of ideas used. It all depends upon what one hopes to get out of this work. One suggestion I might make if the reader begins to feel bogged down is to go back to the very beginning of the Book (or Part, or section) and start over! Back in university I once read a difficult physics chapter well over 15 times and scored highest on the test, in a rather large lecture class; which was a 46% -- perhaps the proudest failure of my life.

> WHAT THE PHILOSOPHERS HAVE SUCCEEDED IN IS THIS:
> THE MORE THEY TALK ABOUT IT
> THE MORE CONFUSED THE PUBLIC BECOMES.
> Lin Yutang
> The Importance Of Living

Thinking is work. Correct thinking is hard work. If one doesn't believe me think back to one's school days when applying himself to learning something new. It was hard. If one still doesn't think that thinking is work it's because he hasn't tried to learn something new lately. As one matures and gets used to good thinking, and more skilled at it, the process gets smoother and quite enjoyable,

4

but the effort of thinking is still there. But there is a pleasure in good thinking and the satisfaction of being an educated person is something that is difficult to put into words.

The purpose of this Book is to help one understand **human** life. If the subject of this work was what is **fundamental** about birds I would now launch into a discussion on the mechanics of flight and how birds achieve it. If this Book were about fish, likewise, I would discuss locomotion through the water. But this Book is about what is fundamental to man, so we will be discussing **the human thinking process.** It is only man for which the thinking process is the fundamental quality that controls his life.   So, really get that! --- ANY improvement in the lot of mankind MUST deal with real improvement the thinking process of somebody. Simply re-arranging institutions, rules, traditions, laws, programs, power factions, protected groups, etc., will never work.

> I WAS BORN NOT KNOWING,
> AND HAVE HAD ONLY A LITTLE
> TIME TO CHANGE THAT HERE AND THERE.
> Richard Feynman

THE BRAIN AND THE MIND

A man is born possessing a computer almost beyond belief were it not for the fact that the operation of such a computer is directly observable by him within himself and in others. (Sad that men pay so much attention to the computer in their lap and not the one in their head.) This computer (the HARDWARE) I am calling the BRAIN. Included in the definition of the brain is the physical plant itself, all the nerve endings and sense-organs, its electro-chemical operation, built-in reflexes, and any innate tendencies built into the individual, such as eating, drinking, sexing, breathing, eliminating, general pleasure seeking and pain avoidance, etc. The brain gathers a wealth of impulses from its environment in the form of what are called "sensations" from the sense organs and musculo-skeletal system -- light, sound, taste, smell, various skin sensations of heat, pressure and pain, the direction of a gravitational field (the three balance canals in the ear area) and the intensity of the field (the "heaviness" felt by the muscles and skeleton of the body). This is the BRAIN.

But the BRAIN (the computer) begins life with no program – it is this PROGRAM that I am calling the MIND. It is the improvement and use of the mind (the program) that this Book primarily concerns. The ultimate goal of the

5

brain is to correctly IDENTIFY everything it encounters, to adequately EVALUATE it, and to adequately RESPOND to it by acquiring a fine working mind. I am going to explain to my readers, as best I can and in my own words, the process by which this is accomplished, as well as some notions of when, and how, the process goes wrong.

Man has both innate tendencies as well as learned ideas and behaviors. I just referred to the more obvious innate tendencies that men do have. Lacking clear evidence regarding the source of a man's behavior, it is important to assume that his mind and volition are at work. Since man's mind is so powerful this is a fair charge simply on principle. However, the practical reason to assume volition is elegantly alluded to in a quote provided by Joseph Weizenbaum in his book, which I will take the liberty of paraphrasing just a bit for brevity and clarity:

> "Suppose we choose between two hypotheses. No matter which one we select, there is always the possibility that the other is correct. Obviously, the likelihood of making a mistake when we select one, or the other, matters ,,,,,,, however, so do the **costs** of making a mistake. We might choose a hypothesis somewhat less likely yet with a smaller cost for being wrong, than the other way around. Such a decision can only be made on the basis of our **values.** For example: consider the view that there are genetic differences in mental functioning between "races." If society adopted this view and it was false, great and unnecessary harm would be done. But conversely, if society adopted the alternative view of no racial differences in mental ability, and it were false, then we would expect much less harm to be done."
>
> Marc J. Roberts
> Harvard economist

Obviously, in the above, even the conclusion of which error would cause the greater harm is also **another value judgement!** There are those who do indeed believe it to be "safer" to assume that the races are different in mental ability, or that rearing environment or culture present **insurmountable** obstacles to equal treatment, and to act on those assumptions, (There's that bogus nature vs. nurture argument again.) The premise of this Book is that without clear evidence to the contrary, it is safer to assume man's volition to be at work. We will proceed to show just what volition is, and why it is imperative to give it its due weight.

6

ASTRONOMY, GEOLOGY , BIOLOGY AND HISTORY ALL PROVIDE
PRETTY GOOD MATERIAL TO HELP US FORM A FAIRLY GOOD
VIEW IF WE DON'T ATTEMPT TOO MUCH AND JUMP AT CONCLUSIONS.
IT DOESN'T MATTER IF, IN THIS BIGGER VIEW OF THE PURPOSE OF THE
CREATION, MAN'S PLACE RECEDES A LITTLE. IT IS ENOUGH THAT HE
HAS A PLACE, AND BY LIVING IN HARMONY WITH THE NATURE AROUND
HIM, HE WILL BE ABLE TO FORM A WORKABLE AND REASONABLE
OUTLOOK ON HUMAN LIFE ITSELF.

Lin Yutang
The Importance Of Living

At birth the brain begins to program itself automatically. If completely left to its own devices, with no attention or care from the consciousness, it will still compile a complete philosophy of life to one's own satisfaction. It will provide for one's base survival under the conditions in which it was formed – one's childhood -- and one will forever seek the living conditions of a child. It will be largely copied from those who cared for oneself , and/or a **reaction to them.** One will be the smartest, most independent thinker in the whole world, needing no advice and seeking none. In conversation with others one will not listen but rather "wait to talk" and learn nothing from anyone or anything. Reading books will be for entertainment mostly, although one may fancy oneself quite the intellectual. If one feels that a certain topic is important, he will consider himself to be an expert on it and his position will be immovable. If some other topic is considered personally irrelevant it will be ignored. One will finally change his position on any important issue if his own life or comfort is at stake, while the lives of others will be negotiable. The rest of this list could be very long, but one gets the idea. So, simply having a **World View** does not necessarily mean that one has accomplished anything at all. Everyone has a world view – and we are looking for something more.

FOR ANYONE WHO HAD EXPERIENCED THE PERFECT UNDERSTANDING
OF ONE THING, AND TRULY TASTED HOW KNOWLEDGE IS ACCOMPLISHED,
WOULD SEE WHAT HE KNOWS AND WHAT HE DOES NOT KNOW.
Galileo Galilei
Dialogue Concerning The Two Chief World Systems

THE CONSCIOUSNESS

The "consciousness" is like a movie screen created by the brain onto which a man's life, (all of his perceptions, thoughts, memories, emotions, etc.) is projected. We have no idea how the consciousness is created, but it allows the brain to "experience" its own existence, and creates a "you" and allows this "you" to participate in the process of mind development. The consciousness allows the brain to interact with both the individual as well as its environment in a very special way.

SENSATIONS and PERCEPTIONS

At birth the brain begins to **program itself.** For about the first two years the process is fairly automatic as there is yet insufficient mind (i.e., first level concepts, memories, etc.) to participate meaningfully in the process. During this time the brain is like a sponge, forming perceptions and what are called **first level concepts,** and establishing the beginnings of a **personality,** largely in response to the child's surroundings, particularly those who care for it. Later on this personality can be adjusted somewhat by the man's thinking processes.

For some time after birth the brain experiences only a mass of color, sound, and other raw inputs called **sensations.** The brain is naturally designed to make sense of this raw input and convert the data into **perceptions.** The eyes learn to focus, the retinas recognize three colors (wavelengths of light) as well as "light or no light", the ears are mechanically designed to favor specific tones (wavelengths of sound), taste and smell buds in the tongue and nose react to certain chemicals, etc. Special areas of the brain seem dedicated to processing the billions, perhaps trillions, of these impulses from the body and they are organized into "perceptions".

At this point it is important to emphasize two things. During the pure perception stage we have not reached the point of "person", "dog", "cat", etc. A perception is merely the "awareness of some separate discreet entity". The second point to make here is the importance of touch. Without reaching out and touching the world about it the brain is not quite sure whether the world it is experiencing is a world of separate entities or just a flat picture of something. So touch seems fundamental and it is questionable whether its absence would allow the existence of any higher animal. So the baby, or child, wants to touch,,,,,, it MUST touch, at least until the world of separate entities is a proven fact. A baby or child not very much into touch is already in for some serious cognitive problems – it is not "curious".

8

FIRST LEVEL CONCEPTS

The next stage of cognitive development is one humans also share with the higher animals. Although undoubtedly an oversimplification of the process, it appears that one striking feature of the brain is that it functions similar to a vast **filing system** with hundreds of filing cabinets, thousands of file drawers, and hundreds of thousands of file folders. Just as in the stage of perception formation, the stage of first level concept formation is fairly automatic and flawless. Everyone pretty much agrees on what is "person", "cat", or "dog". These initial first level concepts are formed by the brain by grouping all entities sharing defining **perceptual characteristics** into a single "file folder", and these file folders we call **first level concepts.**

At this juncture it is appropriate to emphasize a point. We share first level concepts with the higher animals. The higher animals never have a word for "person", "cat", or "dog", just as the very young child does not, but they do recognize the group as such. Though animals never have a word, in the human sense, for a first level concept, they certainly can have a sound for it. When I say "cat!", our dog knows exactly what I'm talking about. At the early first level concept stage a concept is merely a file folder with like objects in it, with no word attached, which the animal can reference when needed; such as in a dog --- "Oh, there is another two-legged object that moves, is friendly to me, and might feed me." Being human, young children quickly move beyond this stage and can name things at will.

Compared to our knowledge of how the **brain** works, we think we have a better handle on how the **mind** works -- functionally. Remember, the mind is not a physical thing, but rather the design of something much like a computer program. In theory we should be able to observe something about how the mind works. This is what we are attempting.

9

BEYOND FIRST LEVEL CONCEPTS

WE OUGHT TO EXPECT REALITY IN MANY CASES
TO BE INVISIBLE, AVAILABLE ONLY TO THOSE
COGNITIVE POWERS THAT GO BEYOND SENSORY PERCEPTION.
Johann Goethe

The land beyond first level concepts is a truly remarkable place. It appears that the human brain has an ability which differs from the other animals. Here we see another uncanny resemblance to the modern digital computer. The field of digital computing has a technology called "data compression". I am not a computer scientist, but the process must work by recognizing repeating patterns in data and then assigning a "shorthand" (probably a number and an associated sequence of data) to every incidence of the repeating data. Then, upon "de-compression", the original information is decoded back into the data prior to music playback, text display, or whatever. But the human brain takes this basic principle much farther. The brain apparently has the ability to recognize **repeating patterns of ideas,** even very subtle patterns not readily available to the consciousness, and "compress" the repeating incidences of them into what we call **higher level concepts.** The concept then comes to represent every incidence of the idea. By our previous analogy, in "first level concepts" the brain established the file **folders** – in "higher level concepts" the brain now builds the file **drawers** and file **cabinets!**

In computing, data compression is for saving storage space; in human reasoning, concepts are for **saving thinking!** (and storage space as well). Here we see the beginnings of the distinction between mere "thinking" and what is to be called **reasoning.** A man might be very busy thinking, yet not be reasoning at all!

Sometimes, but not always, a concept has an attached emotion and a response. In other cases the higher concept is merely a logical "step" in the reasoning process. Afterwards, the trick becomes when to apply which concepts to what external situations – another learned skill of the rational person. Once a set of observations or ideas are **properly** conceptualized they may then be safely relegated to the background of one's knowledge and referred to only as needed.

Strictly speaking, even perceptions and first level concepts are a form of knowledge compression in the brain, but are closer to the data compression of the computer, and again, are shared with the higher animals (and are automatic) -- and so this observation is only made in passing. We may also take note here of common sayings such as, "People use only one tenth of their brains", reflecting the false notion of knowledge that the brain is some kind of vessel into which knowledge is "poured". Not only are such notions an **underestimation of quantity,** but minimize what really matters – man's concept formation.

Next, the brain is able to take its higher level concepts **seriously,** treat them **as percepts** (i.e., not needing further validation), and **cross reference concepts!** So we move from "cat" and "dog" to "animal", which now allows us to distinguish "animal" from "plant". By this **stacking process,** and certainly some other nuances, man is able to perform all the magnificent thinking of which he is capable. When reflecting on the journey from "sensations" to the highest level thinking of which men are capable, and how it appears that the process works, it is impossible to conclude that a person's ancestry, or continent of origin, or their sex, will **pre-determine** how a person thinks or acts. All such things are learned!

I now present an idea on how the brain knows does what it does, and this is little more than an observation on the structure of the **neuron.** I also mention it because I have never seen it explicitly alluded to in my readings. The human brain is the largest to have ever existed and has, on average, an estimated 100 BILLION neurons. This means that there are TRILLIONS of unique connections between brain cells, and many more trillions of possible pathways, and combinations of pathways, within the brain. So I ask, is it possible that every single percept, concept, conclusion, emotion and response that a man holds represents a unique combination of neural pathway within his brain established by the thinking process? If there is anything to this notion it could account for the brain's seeming limitless capacity for learning and understanding, part of the difficulties in changing one's ideas, as well as certain aspects of learning and recovery from minor brain damage.

THINKING AS A GUIDE TO ACTION

Like any other organ of the body, the purpose of the brain is to survive the body. There are no exceptions to this. Any part of an animal's body that is not used for survival or reproduction will atrophy through the process of natural selection. Man's astounding ability to think is a very late comer on the animal

11

scene, and the ability evolved to survive the species under the conditions in which it occurred, prior to our modern world. This is further evidence of the equal **mental potential** of all humans. Our brains evolved for rubbing sticks together to make fire and chipping stones to make arrow heads -- yet some people who, by pure chance, happened to be born in a certain country, landed machines on the Moon! Two men even did it for the very first time, nearly flawlessly. (If the reader has never watched the 15 minute Apollo 11 moon landing video it is highly recommended. In reality, computers are an absolute requirement for the complex calculations and navigation of space travel, but this does not detract from the intelligence, training and chutzpah of the men who pioneered it.)

So thinking is a man's guide to action for his survival –**and is experienced as such by the man!** Due to his nature, and the facts of man's existence, it is a contradiction to not allow man to act on his thinking. At each step of the thinking process, a man's concepts stand for PRINCIPLES for guiding a man in forming CONCLUSIONS to guide his ACTIONS. The method of working through all of these steps is called **logic.** Specifically, the process involves correctly grouping like percepts and/or concepts, identifying them correctly and acting accordingly. At higher levels of reasoning the process is complex and is carried on by the brain only partly consciously. The process proceeds well, or poorly, largely dependent on a man's **intention,** to be fully discussed in Part 3!

So,,, as a teaching aid we will use the following diagram of the thinking process:

(Note: Since sensations and perceptions are FULLY automatic they will
        be omitted from subsequent diagrams – and I will need the space)

But our outline of the thinking process is not complete. There are still two features that must be discussed.

12

VOLITION

> Two brothers were raised by an alcoholic father. One grew up to be an alcoholic
> and when asked what happened, he said, "I watched my father." The other grew
> up having never drank once and when asked why he said, "I watched my father."
> Kirk Franklin

(Note: The following paragraphs make a momentous point)

In my Forward I promised the reader a "volitional" view of man. So what, and where, is man's volition?

Perception and low level concept formation are fairly straightforward. However, once concept formation advances, the differences and similarities among observations become subtle, sometimes very subtle, and the brain is now **manipulating ideas as well.** Hence, in order to make further conceptual progress, an ability to **test** different concept formations, and select good ones, evolved in man's brain. Since the dawn of philosophical inquiry the question of whether man is "free" or "determined" has plagued discussion about him. We will now settle this question.

The dominant impression of man's power of volition, or "free will" is diagramed below:

PREVAILING CONCEPTION OF MAN'S FREE WILL

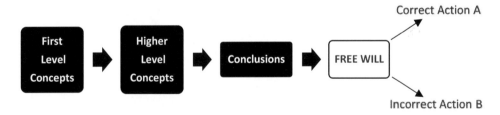

The above policy presumes that whatever trash gets into a man's head, he simply forces himself to "do the right thing" at the end. Therefore, I call this the "will POWER" concept of man's free will, since it takes a lot of POWER to live this way - and it does not work! To those holding the above view of man's volition it does indeed appear that man struggles to be free, since a man's conclusion are in fact the drivers of his actions.

In reality the process works much more like the following:

A MUCH BETTER CONCEPTION OF MAN'S FREE WILL

The above concept of man's freedom of choice recognizes that it is **the ideas a man accepts as true** that primarily forms his conclusions and determines his actions. This is not to say that at the end of the thinking process a man cannot still choose a wrong course of action. It is to say that after a correct reasoning process it will be much easier and likely that he will take the right action. I will say just a bit more on this shortly.

It is by simple introspection that a man identifies his free will. It is obvious to any thinking man that he has control over the ideas he accepts as true and that it is his thinking that leads to his actions. This is the proof.

I close the discussion of volition with an observation regarding those who deny it. Such men will appear, proclaiming the falsity of volition, then attempt to **persuade their audience** (i.e., change their minds and actions!) according to their own social and political views. Let **that** sink in!

EMOTIONS – FOOD FOR THOUGHT

The brain-body is built for its survival around the **pleasure-pain principle.** There are no exceptions to this. For all of its **physical** activities the body has **physical** manifestations of pleasure and pain to cause actions which promote life and avoid destruction. Likewise, the brain, operating on the same principle, has **intellectual** manifestations of pleasure and pain to promote its activities. These intellectual manifestations are called **emotions.**

To fully understand emotions we must consider them from two points of view, which I shall call their **evaluative** aspect and their **function in the thinking process.**

To understand their evaluative aspect we begin with the observation that emotions come in only two kinds -- "good for you", and "bad for you". The brain evaluates its perceptions -- things, situations, even ideas in oneself and others, as either for one's interests or against one's interests, and expresses its conclusion as an **emotion.** We also observe that there is no emoting regarding things that don't interest the individual or affect one in any way, though a man may **fake** having emotions to manipulate situations that DO matter to himself. (Emotions also vary in their **intensity,** but this need not be touched on until later.) We next observe that men frequently make errors in their evaluative conclusions, while the higher animals (within the context of their available information) do not. Men frequently evaluate negatively things that are (ultimately) good for them, and favorably things that are (ultimately) bad for them. People frequently "bite the hand that feeds them", while it is said that dogs do not.

The next significant observation regarding emoting's evaluative aspect is that man emotes regarding himself as well as his surroundings, while the higher animals emote only about their surroundings. Animals do not have volition, at least not the **kind** of volition of man, they cannot change themselves from within, only react to outside stimuli, and so have no need to emote regarding themselves. Humans, on the other hand, are self-starters, can change themselves volitionally, and so do have emotions regarding themselves. We observe that negative feelings about oneself are not intended by nature to be some form of curse or punishment, but as a warning that something is not right – something which the man might be able to correct! A man should try to avoid negative self-emotions about things which he cannot change, but this can certainly at times be difficult.

Lastly, we observe that man also frequently makes errors regarding this aspect of his emotions – he mis-identifies the source of an emotion as either some aspect of himself or his surroundings. In general the pattern among men is to **somewhat** over-identify themselves as the source of their positive emotions ("Look how good I am."), and **grossly** over-identify their environment as the source of their negative emotions ("It's everyone else's fault.").

15

So to sum our observations about emotions:

     1 -- Emotions are of two basic kinds, "good for you" and "bad for you"

     2 -- There are no emotions for things that one thinks irrelevant to oneself

     3 -- Humans emote about themselves as well as their surroundings

     4 -- Men frequently make errors in all aspects of their emotions

     5 -- Men sometimes fake emoting to manipulate situations

     6 -- A man should not automatically trust his emotions

So, as another teaching aid we offer the following diagram of the emoting process:

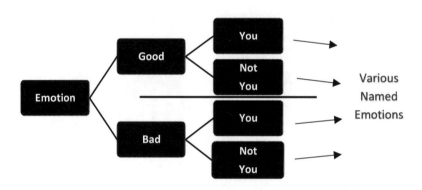

The above diagram is an invaluable tool for understanding one's emotions, evaluating them, understanding if they are honest emotions, etc. For example, try running "jealousy" through the above matrix to see what happens --kind of stuck huh? Jealousy isn't even an honest emotion, or perhaps I should say that the emotion itself may be honest, but that men's definition of it is intentionally sloppy in order to cover up their true motives. Jealousy is really simple **anger** – but anger at what? (Note: I distinguish "jealousy" from "envy", with jealousy being an attitude of possessiveness or ownership towards one's closer relations, and envy being over other people's good fortunes.)

16

The second major perspective regarding emotions is their **role in the thinking process**. Again, emotions play two roles here: as **direct motivators**, and as a **reward or warning** of successful/unsuccessful action. In the opening of this Topic I pointed out that emotions are man's intellectual manifestations of pleasure or pain to motivate and reward man's thinking process. Emotions are man's "food for thought".

Another teaching diagram of the thinking process will best show this role of emotions as direct motivators and reward/warning feelings:

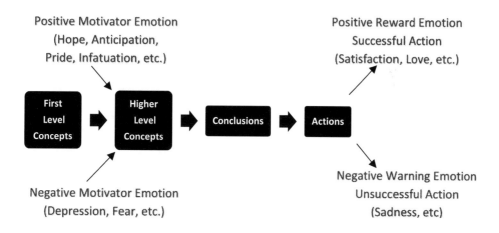

We note that a man's "motivator" emotions do not come out of nowhere but largely from his previous thought processes, and his successes and failures. A most widespread error regarding "reward" emotions is that we simply engage in our actions in pursuit of pleasant emotions. Although in a superficial sense this is true, on a deeper level our actions are not **true cause** in our happiness – it is our **thinking** that is true cause. So a better concept of the process is that our emotions are to encourage us to better thinking. Our emotions are our "food for thought". Therefore the question for you is -- do your emotions work for you, or do you work for them?

So we have the following streamlined teaching diagram showing the **complete thinking process:**

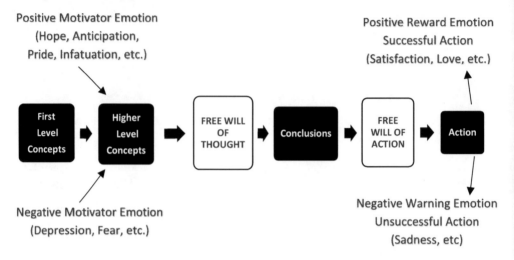

Still, in the above diagram, the "free will of action" step is mostly an illusion. In reality it is a "re-consideration" by the free will of thought. There is no direct line of connection from perceptions, through "free will of action", and thence to one's muscles. The path is through one's conclusions.

So, in the proper conception of the thinking process, the brain performs the electro-chemical integrations of the thinking process, directed by the mind with the faculty of free will (volition), fueled by the emotions. Note from this discussion that the closest a man ever comes to "feeling" his way to the good things in life is the **motivation to begin the journey!** The actual act of achievement is preceded by a process of thought.

So I make the following startling assertions! : Man's free will **IS** his capacity to reason at the level above other animals. They are one and the same. Free will is primarily operative in the ideas that a man accepts as true. Furthermore, since thinking is man's guide to action it follows that man must be free in action as he is free in thought. This is not to say that a man shouldn't be responsible for the **results** of his actions, but that he has the right to perform them – other would be a contradiction.

For simplicities sake I have stated at several points that man is the only animal capable of thinking beyond first level concepts – that all other animals are limited to first level concepts only. Strictly speaking, this cannot be true. Close observation of even the pet dog shows that he is responding to something beyond first level concepts and exercising some choice. The dog does not go to drink every time he looks at his water bowl, nor does he bring me his ball to play every time he sees it. On the other hand he will, at times, actively look for the ball and place it at my feet. Likewise, it is undoubtedly somewhat disconcerting to consider how far our cousins, the chimps and gorillas, take things. Therefore, the remaining differences between humans and higher animals seem to be thus: **1)** Animals cannot manipulate ideas and so, within the context of their available information, they do not make mistakes as humans do, and cannot change themselves from within, and so emote only regarding their surroundings, and **2)** Animals reach the limit of their **conception** before they reach the limit of their **perception**, while man (some men) understands everything he perceives, then makes microscopes, telescopes, scientific and psychological theories, etc., and any number of other clever devices, to detect things not normally perceived, to understand even more. It thus might be said that animals operate at the level of "mere preference", while man is able to conceptualize upon what "ought" to be.

(Before moving on, the reader might consider a change of gears and find the Wikipedia page for "logical fallacies" or "fallacies", and study all the tricks and deceptions that our **minds** play on our **brains!**)

SOME IMPORTANT POINTS REGARDING CONCEPTUAL THINKING

> Mr. Spock: That was some impeccable logic you used to destroy NOMAD, captain.
> Cap. Kirk : You didn't think I had it in me, did you Spock?
> Mr. Spock: Correct captain.
> STAR TREK

> I DO NOT THINK THAT THE SAME GOD
> THAT GAVE US OUR SENSES, INTELLIGENCE,
> AND REASON WISHES US TO
> ABANDON THEIR USE.
> Galileo
> "The Trial Of Galileo"

It should be clear by now that unflappable characters, such as Mr. Spock from Star Trek, are not exactly what is meant by rationality. If anything it was Kirk that better displayed what might be called rationality – although if it weren't for his gullibility getting them into trouble in so many episodes, there might not have been a series. Kirk seemed awfully reckless with that transporter as well as general security. But the bottom line is that man is not faced with the choice of emotion **OR** rationality. The rational man keeps all aspects of his thinking in their proper perspective.

It was previously theorized that among the higher animals the practical limit of their brain's abilities is to group perceptions to form first level concepts, while man's brain achieves a much higher intelligence by grouping concepts into ever higher concepts, treating concepts as if they were percepts, and stacking and cross referencing concepts. It must now be understood that man's conceptual faculty works well only if his structure of concepts is built correctly, and concepts are taken **seriously.** This is called "thinking in principles", or "logic".

A simple outline of logical thinking will illustrate the process. Consider sets of observations A and B, each of which is always seen to be true, i.e., they are "conceptualized". It is further observed that Observations A and B always have a bearing on a Problem C. Problem C can be anything from an action we wish to take to a concept we wish to formulate.   A diagram as an aid is offered below:

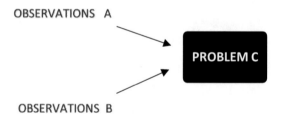

Therefore, the rules of logic dictate that Problem C must **NEVER** be solved in a way that contradicts or violates Observations A and B, or any other facts or validated concepts that have a bearing on Problem C. In other words a solution to Problem C must **conform to the facts of reality,** otherwise it is not a solution, but a confusion.

In practical terms, as affecting the world in which we live, it would be much better to live in a world with men who accept the logic and inevitable solution to Problem C while simply saying that they are unwilling to "go that far right now", than to attempt to argue with the kind of people who do not deal in logical conclusions to begin with.   There will be more to say about such "Intellectual Honesty" later.

Contrast logical thinking with the approach of the **irrational** man who sees Observations A and B as **obstacles** to solving Problem C, since the solution must conform to them, (a manifestation of the problem oriented thinking from the Forward of this Book). But the rational man has a completely different attitude. To him, Observations A and B **assist** in the solution of Problem C, since they point to answers that might, or might not, work – and may rule out things that would certainly not work.

At this juncture we also point out one of the most important maxims of all philosophy: That "**the burden of proof is on he who asserts the positive**". What this means is that it is impossible to prove that something does **not** exist, or that something did **not** happen, or that some action should **not** be taken; and it is generally an error to ask for, to expect, or to **attempt to give** such proof. For example, if an action is proposed it is the proponent(s) of the action on whom the burden falls to show the likely benefits of the action and/or how similar actions in the past have succeeded (in the long term view). When the detractors of the proposal point out the likely negative consequences of the plan this does not mean that they are "trying to prove their negative". Furthermore, any existing problems cannot automatically be pinned onto any "inaction", for this would be still another "positive" to be proven. So it could be said that, in this limited sense, "The Man Who Only Sits, Is Right".

And finally, it is not necessary, nor possible, for a man to be fully conscious of his entire thinking process. What is necessary is for a man to have the **intention** to reason and accept the right ideas as true – the brain will accomplish most of the rest. More about this in the next Part.

I will share an example from my own life to help illustrate the power of conceptual thinking. The vast majority of students in school will "take notes" in class – writing down what the instructor says. I too did this, for a couple of years in university. But one day I simply put my pen down and never picked it up again – after all, what are those outrageously priced textbooks for, right? So there I was, perhaps the only young person in class just sitting there watching the teacher, everyone else busily writing. I could never have put that pen down without a confidence in conceptual thinking. I was not at the time fully conscious of what I was doing. My working theory was that understanding the material, working the problems, and studying the text would carry me. I can just hear my teachers in their break room, commenting, "Mr. Choate has stopped taking notes." There are some subjects, history for one example, which have some things to simply memorize -- dates for example. But one also finds subjects that have either not been properly conceptualized, **cannot** be properly conceptualized, or else has a sicko teacher who **will not** conceptualize the subject and is "playing games" with the students, forcing them to take notes lest they miss some obscure point – which, of course, he makes a point of asking on the test. (Now we're really getting into the "meat" of this Book!)

HIS HEAD WAS AN HOURGLASS.
IT COULD STOW AN IDEA,
BUT IT HAD TO DO IT ONE GRAIN AT A TIME.
Mark Twain

Memorization and conceptualization are quite different things. Both have their place in thinking, but conceptualization is "higher", i.e., more "human", and therefore more difficult in a certain sense. Consequently there are men who go through life attempting to "memorize it". This can only take one so far. In fact, it is not unknown for extremely intelligent, successful people, (often males who must go out into the world to "make the bacon"), to simply "lose it' (give up) sometime in the middle of life, (say in their 40's). It is possible that a contributing factor for these people is that they are highly **non-conceptual** and the complexity of life just catches up with them.

The recent, so called, **Common Core** math for young people is another illustration – it is the attempt to remove **both** memorization and conceptualization from basic mathematics, reducing it to **pure perception,** as in an animal. There is no way that a person can take this type of math to the next level. The more intelligent students have the most trouble with the approach. To put it kindly, and giving the greatest benefit of the doubt, it is the attempt to give the least (intelligently) fortunate students the best chance to compete with their betters.

In 1988, I was sitting for my test to become an engineer. It is an open book test and some people bring many books – some need a cart or dolly to carry their stacks of books – yet there I was, sitting there with my little pile of books, (no one uses much of the books he brings). Then, filling out the personal information on the test cover sheet, I had this little problem of not remembering my own name!..... disconcerting for one who is about to take the test of his life. Now, you can call this being scared "whit-less" over a test if you like -- but I wasn't scared to put that pen down back in school, was I? I prefer the interpretation that my mind had simply prepared me for the highest conceptual performance that it could, and was just not, at that particular moment, into recalling things that I had memorized. So anyway, I passed the test (probably by the skin of my teeth). It was my first try, and the pass rate for that cycle was about 45% (45% of testees passed). The test is harder these days and so are the available study materials.

Another nice passage from Joseph Weizenbaum's, Computer Power And Human Reason, reinforces the present discussion and points toward the importance of conceptualization:

> "Students sometimes prepare themselves for examinations in physics by memorizing lists of equations. They may well pass their examinations with the aid of such feats of memory, but it can hardly be said that they know physics. A good theory is thus not merely a kind of data bank in which one can "look up" what would happen under such and such conditions. It is rather like a map of partially explored territory. The way that theories make a difference in the world is not merely that they answer questions but that they guide further intelligent search."

One final observation, for example, would be that most young students find basic chemistry to be easier than basic physics, or at least more pleasant. This is why chemistry has traditionally been presented to high school juniors, while physics to the seniors. The reason is because basic chemistry lends itself better to memorization techniques, while physics forces a more conceptual approach early on.

SIMPLE IDEAS NOT RIGHT OR WRONG
Good thinking includes something like the, so called, "brain storming" practice used by organizations in group discussions. (It is interesting, psychologically, how the value of this is recognized for group settings but not so much for the individual. More about this later.) The rational man's mind is active and will experience a constant flow of ideas of all kinds. Whether an idea is "true" or "false" is only to be determined by a careful accounting of all known, related facts. Once an idea is determined as "true", it must still be inserted correctly into a man's concept structure. A simple idea is not **cognitively wrong** until it is erroneously used. The rational man wants to understand life and part of this achievement lies in his not censoring his simple ideas.

23

It cannot be overemphasized that thinking in principles gets its value and power from the concept structure being built correctly. The concepts must be "valid", i.e. must conform to reality; they must be logical, i.e. not contradictory within themselves; they must be developed as consciously as possible and remain so, at least until they are adequately validated and automatized; and one's principles must be taken seriously – they must be trusted, and they must be used as guides for action. To deny that principles are necessary guides to thinking and action is to say that man cannot make sense of his world.

Sometimes one hears of "consciousness expanding" and of various techniques or theories of how this might be realized. These efforts claim to have in common the hope of helping people be more successful at living and/or getting more enjoyment out of life. The fact is that there is only one way to "expand one's consciousness", and that is by enriching an impoverished brain/mind with better ideas, principles, and conclusions, improving one's relationship with one's emotions, and taking action. There are no short cuts to this – there is only the long cut of reasoning. However, that being said, my laying all this stuff out like this could save a fellow a lot of running around, don't you think?

> EVEN THOUGH I DON'T THINK I'LL CONVERT THE WORLD
> TO RATIONALITY, I MAY INFLUENCE AN OCCASIONAL PERSON
> HERE AND THERE; AND ANY ADDITION TO THE TOTAL OF
> RATIONALITY IS PRECIOUS.
> Isaac Asimov

BREAKTHROUGH MOMENTS or "CONCEPTUAL JUMPS"

Depending on one's starting point upon reading this Volume, and if one is very observant, and very fortunate, one may experience a **Breakthrough Moment.** The moment consists of a self-reflection that some kind of "**conceptual jump**" has occurred in the brain, along with an accompanying emotion. The observation means that the brain is now beginning to think with a greater number of supporting concepts **simultaneously,** along with the accompanying emotion of **satisfaction.** The man is now "wiser" than he was before. The moment is deeply satisfying, fleeting, and, sadly, should only be available to any man two or three times in his life, at most. I have noticed only one.

Finally, some important points must be covered. The more observant among my readers will recall that I made the following assertions, either explicitly or implicitly:

1 -- Man's brain/mind, as well as his physical pleasures and discomforts, and emotions are directed toward the survival of his physical body. I claimed that they exist for no other purpose. That the consciousness can enjoy physical pleasure and pleasant emotions is merely an incidental "trick" played on the consciousness, by the body, to cause the efforts directed at survival.

2 -- A man always interprets physical pleasure (when experienced) and positive emotions (when experienced) as being good for him (i.e., life promoting), and physical discomfort (when experienced) and negative emotions (when experienced) as being bad for him (i.e., life damaging).

3 -- Man's brain will always seek out physical pleasure and positive emotions.

So again, the more observant (and skeptical) of my readers may suspect that our reasoning is circular or that we are promoting some kind of cynical or hedonistic way of life, and be asking the following questions:

1 -- So what is the meaning of life if the whole point is simply to cause survival of the body?

2 -- Since some things that feel good are bad for you, and some things that are good for you are unpleasant in the short term, how is one to consistently seek out the good without just guessing?

In answer to Question 1, recall that the conclusions of Metaphysics require us first to accept the universe as it exists, without question – it just is! Recall also that we have no idea how the consciousness is created -- it just is! We simply accept that we seek out the things in life that cause our happiness and be happy. We don't "over think" the issue. **THAT** is the meaning of life. And this is not cynical – it just is what it is. We must understand that the meaning of life can only be what man can reason out with his mind. Living life requires that we know when to stop thinking and start living.

The second question too is fair enough. Part of the answer lies in the following observation. If I stand at the edge of a cliff I will not attempt to walk out into thin air (unless I'm a coyote), nor do the vast majority of other humans or higher animals, for our PERCEPTUAL mentalities can predict what will happen. This prediction is learned through the many previous smaller observations, so that, hopefully, the BIG mistake is avoided. What most men do not understand is that the CONCEPTUAL mentality (when well developed) is also quite capable of predicting the consequences of policies and actions. The problem is that many men do not have a well-developed conceptual mentality. Granted, the **conceptual predictions** made by the mind/brain are necessarily more nebulous than perceptual predictions, but this does not render them invalid or useless. As vague as conceptual predictions can be, a novel was completed in 1957, which included such things (among many others) as social take-over of health care (it happened), social control of lending practices (it happened), and prohibitions on companies re-locating out of states where they are doing business (it happened – Boeing in Seattle, Washington). The rational man does not decide what to do based simply on what he thinks will feel good. He does it with a process of reason – and feels that!

Another part of the answer is in men's failing to take a LONG RANGE point of view. In the short term some bad things may be attractive, and some good things, unpleasant. But the rational man minimizes these apparent conflicts by taking a long range point of view. By reasoning things "all the way through" most conflicts between what is good and what a man feels like doing can be reconciled.

So we do not promote a hedonistic way of life, nor suggest living life as a monk. We promote happiness through reason. If one doubts that there is an effective way of living, one need only look around at people and see the great variety of skill levels at the task. Regardless of whether these observations and suggestions of mine are perfect in every way, I can personally attest to their value.

In this Part we theorized that it is the brain's "program" (the mind) which directs a man's thinking process. We now turn to the question: **By what rules ought the mind direct the brains thinking process?** This is the subject of Ethics – the study of a man in relation to himself.

What follows is my "spin" on the subjects of ethics and politics from a slightly more psychological angle, and is only meant as a summary and to present some novel ideas I have had on the subjects. My purpose is to provide guidance to men in the **application of a philosophy to their own lives.** The reader is encouraged to refer to materials listed in the Resource And Example Reading List, to find other accounts of philosophy, including ethics and politics.

PART 3: ETHICS
(The Normal Psychology Of The Individual <u>NOT</u> In Relation To Others)

LET HIM THAT WOULD MOVE THE WORLD
FIRST MOVE HIMSELF
Socrates

In this Part, and the next, I use the term "normal" in the subtitles, therefore I must define what I mean by that. By this term I mean to say that a man in question has a **physiologically** normally functioning brain, and that the man has not been excessively **psychologically** damaged beyond repair as a child, thus destroying the person's very ability to think through problems at all. In other words, this entire Volume presumes a man with a properly functioning BRAIN and a MIND that has not been excessively damaged by his growing environment. Up to this point the discussion has been about what men have in common – what makes men the same. We now turn to the things that set men apart.

Life is unavoidably a series of problems to be solved. This is the subject of **Ethics.** I use the term "problems" here in the widest possible sense – encompassing all of the issues men face in life, the unexpected as well as the expected, in acquiring the things men want and need to survive and be happy. The better one gets at dealing with life's problems the happier one should be. When we look at all of the problems that life can throw at men, we can use the epistemological process outlined in Part 2 to integrate (condense) all of these problems down to **three fundamental ones** that all men must face. It is from these three problems that all other specific **man-made** problems issue forth.

(Note: The importance of the following paragraphs cannot be overstated.)

Recall that in Part 2 it was theorized that the integration of sensations into perceptions is accomplished automatically by the brain, and that the integration of perceptions into first level concepts is also very straightforward, essentially automatic. At that point, if it were possible for the brain to take its time to **slowly** develop higher level concepts, **independently,** by its own observations, the

29

process might proceed more or less splendidly and we might all end up as "Aristotles", so to speak. However, this would not be acceptable. Time is of the essence as the child is growing up and must possess enough concepts to survive in the world. The process could never be completed on time if the child's brain had to independently discover every new concept and properly integrate it with all of its ascendant concepts. Therefore, for better or worse, the child's brain has a shortcut – copying!

The child's brain observes the ideas, opinions, manners and methods of the people around it, primarily its caretakers, treats the material **as first level concepts** (i.e., not needing validation), **copies it**, and starts to **think with it!** The copying is imperfect at best, and the material has not been properly integrated with the child's existing percepts and first level concepts (which are correct), is not properly anchored to them, and so is not usable **for the development of reasoning.** Furthermore, the quality of thinking that exists in the world is abysmally poor, and so the most crucial of the new copied material is **false,** rife with contradictions, and will not agree with the child's existing perceptions and simple concepts. In general, the more important is the copied material the **more likely it is to be false** (why else would the world be so screwed up?). If man still existed at the animal level this simple copying of ideas would be adequate for his survival, but due to human volition it is **not even sufficient for that**, much less for his happiness.

In order to accept the copied contradictory material the child must become a **liar.** In many cases ideas are imposed onto the child, by the older people, by subtle messaging, or in other cases more openly by physically or psychologically brutal means (eg., "you will go to hell", "we won't love you", etc.) Such caretakers may **outwardly** display unconditional acceptance of the child, particularly as the child gets a little older and achieves a **psychological maturity** approximately equal to that of the caretaker.

But the damage has already been done – the true purpose was not so much to control the child's actions as to destroy his rationality – leaving the caretaker's own irrationality safe and unexposed. Should he grow up to display actions approved of by the caretakers, he is "right"; if he differs, he is "wrong". What is most unacceptable is for the child to grow up **different and know what he is**

doing! The greatest hatred (and least compassion) for men is reserved not for the misfits who are lost ("Poor man,,,, and besides he's sorry for going against us."), but for the **un-repentant non-conformists** who "do it their way", yet are successful, happy, competent. The greatest damage done to children is not mistakes presented as mistakes, but intellectual error presented as truth!

As psychologically traumatic as the described process must be to the child's brain, he has **no memory** of it. None of us do. And if there is anything in a person's life of which he has no memory that turns out later on to be a problem, then THAT is a BIG problem! Lastly, once the child gets comfortable living with contradictions (intellectual lies) this usually becomes a way of life for the person. So we have been describing the first fundamental problem faced by all men:

PROBLEM 1: INTELLECTUAL DEPENDENCY

Once intellectual dependency has become a habit for the child/young person it is all downhill so to speak, intellectually, for the person. Most men do not realize the extent to which they have simply borrowed, from other men, their ideas, opinions, positions. With all of the important people in a person's life telling him both what and how to think, of what use is it for the brain to gather information, think for itself, etc.? Such new information and original thinking would only conflict with the required dictates anyway -- so why bother? And again, in some cases a prohibition on gathering information and original thinking is imposed on the person by others by **physically or psychologically brutal means.** And so we have the second fundamental problem faced by all men:

PROBLEM 2: INTELLECTUAL DULLNESS / LAZINESS

This is not to say that all men are intellectually dull or lazy, though most men could use some improvement. It is to say that it is an issue that all men must face.

People complain that so many children are not learning in school and can't "think critically". An educational system, to be effective, consists of three elements, all of which must function well – **1)** Some kind of curriculum and a learning environment, **2)** Traditionally some kind of teacher or facilitator, and **3)** A student willing and able to learn. The fact is that long before they enter any formal school most children have already had their ability to reason, and desire for knowledge, significantly damaged by their growing environment!

Finally, I have already mentioned how this whole rickety house is held together – by becoming a liar -- the holding of un-integrated, contradictory concepts. And so we have the final fundamental problem faced by all men:

PROBLEM 3: INTELLECTUAL DISHONESTY

Again, this is not to say that all men are extremely intellectually dishonest, but most are to a greater or lesser degree, and it is an issue that all men must struggle with. A man will not be intellectually dishonest on everything, but only the most crucial issues -- just as a murderer does not kill every person he meets, but only those who interfere with his designs. Included in intellectual dishonesty are common false "fronts" such as various expressions of **intellectual agnosticism** (that ideas don't matter), **promiscuity** (giving up one's ideas too readily), and **egalitarianism** (that one idea is as good as another). In reality these appearances are not true positions held by men, but rather "poses" used in the hope of disarming their opponents by playing off their (the opponent's) guilt, naivete' or good will. In reality **almost no one thinks that their own ideas don't matter, would give them up readily, or that the ideas of others are as good as theirs.**

The reader is again encouraged to refer to a list of "logical fallacies", such as found on Wikipedia, to familiarize himself with the various forms with which intellectual dishonesty expresses itself. Sad that the same "experts" who have done such a complete job of identifying logical error so often deal in those very errors!

THE FIRST PRINCIPLE IS THAT YOU MUST NOT FOOL YOURSELF,
AND YOU ARE THE EASIEST PERSON TO FOOL.
Richard Feynman

As an aid to teaching, the following chart is offered:

THE GOOD (The Primary Virtues)	DESCRIPTION/EXAMPLES	THE EVIL (The Primary Vices)
Intellectual Independence (Courage)	Thinking for oneself. Not accepting anything on faith. "Because I said so", doesn't go. Groups are secondary to the individual.	**Intellectual Dependence** Fear of others. Going along with the crowd, etc.
Intellectual Curiosity (Intelligence)	Gaining knowledge on a variety of topics. Having a variety of interests. (see reading list in back of book) Love of learning, thinking	**Intellectual Dullness/Laziness** Difficulty in learning, easily bored, poor coping skills, easily stressed, etc., materialism, addictions
Intellectual Honesty (Conscience)	The refusal to hold contradictory ideas. The world makes sense-only man creates confusion. Do I have enough knowledge to justify a conclusion? Have other people unduly influenced my conclusions?	**Intellectual Dishonesty** Hypocrisy, Lying, Cheating, Stealing, etc., Guilty feelings, trouble sleeping, Addictions

Since life is largely a series of problems to be solved, and solving problems is the means to achieving the good things in life, we shall call the means of overcoming life's problems **"virtue"**, and **"vice"** the means of succumbing to them.

VISION WILL NOT BE LIMITED SO MUCH BY WHAT IS SEEN
AS BY THE MIND BEHIND THE EYE THAT SEES IT.
Guy Murchie

BRIEF ELABORATIONS ON THE PRIMARY VIRTUES

Let us discuss the **Primary Virtues** in more detail to make clear what it means to live by them. Each of the virtues implies both thought **and** action, since thought is man's guide **to** action.

The virtue of Intellectual Independence, **(Courage),** means that a man thinks for himself and lives according to his conclusions. He considers himself first and foremost a member of the group "human beings", and strives for his own perfection. Then he sees himself as a citizen of a country in which he hopes, and strives, that all men might someday be free. He cares about the opinions of others since he must live with them, he likes and loves some of them, has much to learn from them, and benefits from their association in many ways; but still, he is the responsible party – the buck stops with him. HE must decipher what is true and act on it. He knows that learning from others, both from their successes as well as their mistakes, is an important aspect of Intellectual Independence. He is careful as to what formal or informal associations he joins. He knows that, as things stand presently, any group of more than a few people will likely include evil people with dark motives. Accordingly he tends to choose associations with very focused goals, and monitors any drift away from the stated goals. These are some of the many qualities of the intellectually independent man. This Volume is filled with examples of intellectually independent thinking to help the reader become more skilled and comfortable with this mental state.

> My son Richard is finishing his schooling here (at M.I.T) next Spring. Now he tells me he wants to go on to do more studying, to get still another degree (at Princeton). I guess I can afford to pay his way for another three or four years. But what I want to know is, is it worth it for him? He tells me you've been working with him. Is he good enough to deserve the extra schooling?
>> GENIUS: The Life And Science
>> Of Richard Feynman
>> James Gleick

> IT IS VERY BRASH TO CONSIDER EVERYTHING IN THE UNIVERSE SUPERFLUOUS THAT WE DO NOT IMMEDIATELY UNDERSTAND TO HAVE BEEN CREATED FOR US.
>> Galileo Galilei
>> Dialogue Concerning The Two Chief World Systems

The virtue of Intellectual Curiosity, **(Intelligence),** means that a man wants to understand the world around him, including the people in the world and their actions. If a man is going to think independently he will need a good deal of facts and information **to think with!** To quote, once again, from Joseph Weizenbaum's book: "I shall argue that an entirely too simplistic notion of intelligence has dominated both popular and scientific thought." The intellectually curious man loves nature and wants to master it and deal successfully with it. He knows that all knowledge is connected, and so understanding "one thing" helps him understand all things. He is knowledgeable about his chosen career and his hobbies, but not only about those things. He need not be interested in everything, but is interested in a **variety of things, in several fields.** He need not be an expert in all his fields of interest, but his knowledge could not be termed merely "superficial" either – he takes care to not spread himself too thin, as his time is limited. He is not easily bored, as his mind is a playground of ideas. As he lives his life, his useful intelligence steadily increases – though his physical powers may wane, his mental powers rise. He is a faithful reader and takes great pleasure in experiencing the reasonable ideas of others. His concern about an idea is not of who thought of it, but -- is it true? These are some of the many qualities of the intellectually curious man. This Volume is filled with examples of intellectually curious thinking to help the reader become more skilled and comfortable with this mental state.

> One of my earliest impressions of grown-ups, in general,
> was that they were liars, saying not what they thought or felt,
> but what they believed would serve some particular purpose.
> Nathaniel Branden
> Judgement Day: My Years With Ayn Rand

THE TRUTH HAS A CERTAIN RING TO IT
Ernest Hemingway

The essence of the virtue of Intellectual Honesty, **(Conscience),** is the stand that there are no contradictions in nature; that only man creates confusion, problems. A **stand** is not a platitude one merely recites and then does not act on, but something one **lives.** A man cannot make sense of himself or of the World unless and until he thinks **that such sense can be made!** The virtue of Intellectual Honesty means that a man fights against contradictions in his thinking, conclusions, and actions. He is "honest" in both thought and deed. He becomes

35

skillful in judging his sources of information. He takes care in having adequate knowledge about any subject on which he takes a strong position – particularly if his position affects any other person. He is rare in that he readily gives up his positions for better positions, or if he sees he is mistaken. He wants not to be "right", but **correct!** He can be counted on to do his assigned tasks well, and takes personal satisfaction in a job well done. He loves admiring his work. He is his own best critic. He remembers his mistakes as well, or better than his successes. These are some of the many qualities of the intellectually honest man. This Volume is filled with examples of intellectually honest thinking to help the reader become more skilled and comfortable with this mental state.

> WHY DOEST THOU CONCERN THYSELF WITH THE
> MOTE IN THY NEIGHBOR'S EYE WHEN THOU DOEST
> HAVE A PLANK IN THINE OWN EYE?
> Jesus

Complete Intellectual Honesty is very difficult to achieve, and a man is to be commended for his sincere attempts to live it. One major benefit of a man's association with others is the receiving of their ideas in order to assist in his own Intellectual Honesty. A man's first priority in his dealings with others must always be his own honesty. Another important quality for one's Intellectual Honesty is that of "self-reflection", or "self-objectification" -- the attempt to step outside of oneself and see one's ideas "merely for what they are", or to see ourselves "as others see us" – a skill very difficult to practice. To illustrate these points I offer the following real-life example: If I am talking with a man who is speaking in error, (and if I'm behaving myself), I should be at least as interested in fully understanding the error as in trying to correct him. Not only would this be the right thing for myself, but it is highly unlikely that he is interested in correction, and in fact, the greater the error the less likely his interest.

> A hypocrite is a caught liar. He maintains his hypocrisy by denying,
> through his behavior, the lie of which he has been convicted. Hypocrisy
> is the most vicious mechanism of which the mind is capable, and the one
> against which Christ brought the full and continuing pressure of his arguments.
> Philip Wylie
> Generation Of Vipers

So we have condensed all possible problems a man can face into three categories, corresponding to the three fundamental existents we find in the World: **1)** The minds of OTHER men, **2)** Existence itself, and **3)** A man's OWN mind. All of a man's problems **not in relation to other men** can be traced back to the failure to deal with these three existents. This is not to say that a man is always morally deficient in not meeting life's challenges. Sometimes a man is overwhelmed, through no fault of his own, by the conditions of life. Nevertheless, these are the classes of problems that men face, and each requires its own unique **mental state** to address it. If the challenges of life are going to be met it is **only** the Primary Virtues, and their derivative virtues, that will overcome them.

Please understand that the Primary Virtues ARE mental states and not actions, nor even simple ideas! – they are **ways of being.** Man's actions spring forth from his thinking. Just as man's problems are primarily intellectual, so are his solutions.

The common understanding of the field of ethics is that it is about how we treat others. But our relations with others are only secondary to our own mental state – so understanding man as an individual is prerequisite to the study of man's relation to others. The study of what is right for a man, **as an individual**, is Ethics.

> THE FACULTY BY WHICH MAN LEARNS IS LIKE AN EYE
> WHICH CANNOT BE TURNED FROM DARKNESS TO LIGHT
> UNLESS THE WHOLE BODY BE TURNED.
> IN THE SAME WAY, THE MIND **AS A WHOLE**
> MUST BE TURNED AWAY FROM THE WORLD OF CONFUSION
> BEFORE IT CAN BEAR TO LOOK STRAIGHT AT REALITY,
> AND THAT BRIGHTEST REALITIES, THE GOOD.
> Plato

Virtue is the means to achieving the good things that make life worth living. The thought processes of the Primary Virtues form a unity. It is useful to separate the Virtues for study and self-improvement, but near impossible to actually practice any particular one well without practicing them all well. The attempt to practice any one Virtue without the others will normally lead to moral disaster. (Plato above: The Mind **as a whole** must be turned). For example, if one thinks that the practice of only Intellectual Independence is sufficient, we will end up with a " rebel without a cause". I leave it as an exercise for the reader to think of what the attempted practice of only Intellectual Curiosity might look like (a certain profession seems heavily loaded with this type). As an example of Intellectual Honesty attempted alone we might point to a preacher – he "honestly" tells his congregation **exactly** what they want to hear (intellectual dependency), and **only** what they want to hear (intellectual dullness, laziness).

In the rational man all three mental states will be present at all times, at least in the background, ready to be called up and practiced when needed. The rational man's mind is very active and spends a good deal of time in the "curious" mode, even when interacting with others -- the other virtues are called up as needed.

Another error would be to think that a compromise is possible in the practice of virtue. The following considerations will show why this isn't so. Suppose one follows the policy of practicing Intellectual Independence **sometimes.** In such an example it is readily shown that independence will be practiced when it is convenient, painless, and irrelevant – then, just when independence is difficult, needed, and will matter, one will cave in. Needless to say, this is not Intellectual Independence at all. Precisely the same argument applies to the practice of the remaining Virtues. In fact, it is more difficult to "straddle the fence" in the practice of Virtue than to just go either way. Indeed, in my interactions I do not recall ever meeting anyone I would truly call a straddler – the individual always "bombs" on at least one straightforward issue.

> THE GERMAN PEOPLE DIDN'T REALLY FOLLOW
> HITLER, OR EVEN THE NAZI PARTY;
> THEY FOLLOWED EACH OTHER ---
> UNTIL IT WAS TOO LATE.
> The Author

Though they can only be practiced consistently as a unity, I have debated with myself as to whether any of the Primary Virtues and Vices were more fundamental or important than the others. The best answer I have come up with is that **Intellectual Independence or Dependence seems to be the controlling mentality.** Independence is the easiest mental state to actually practice, but the most difficult one to **choose** to practice, for it immediately places one out of agreement with others, yet one lacks the understanding and conviction needed to stand alone. Once the firm decision is made to be independent, that virtue goes fairly well. By contrast, the other Virtues are easy to choose to practice but harder to actually practice. There are men who buy many books yet never read them, and other men who would never lie to others for the lies they tell themselves are more than adequate.

The prospect of practicing any virtue with little skills in the others causes **acute fear and pain** in the individual. It is as if the person is locked inside a box with the instructions for getting out of the box written on the **outside** of the box, (idea from Dr. Ron Smothermon). Faced with such a dilemma the only place to start might be Intellectual Curiosity, i.e. improving one's factual knowledge -- privately. This might give the individual enough understanding to overcome the other vices. But again, the **other vices will attempt to interfere with the very knowledge one will seek!**

When the child is very young it accepts intellectual dependence, as it almost inevitably must. The child gets used to the "wound" and grows with it. It is easy to grow this way – the "big people" seem to like the compliant child. In truth, it would be just as "natural" for an older child to **outgrow** Intellectual Dependence as it was to accept it as an infant; however, this is not what the "big people" have in mind.

As the child grows he will, of course, make mistakes. Mistakes that may be associated with attempted compliance are termed "Oh look how cute!", while those made out of attempted independence will be punished. In fact it **is the attempted independence** that is being punished. This pattern of forgiveness/punishment continues throughout a persons' life. For all the claims by caretakers of wanting a "better life" for their protégés, this is usually meant in the materialistic sense of better formal education and economic success; few caretakers actually want their charges to become more **rational** than themselves.

In the child the malady is simple Intellectual Dependence, however, in the adult the affliction has metastasized full blown into what is called **Collectivism.** In place of what was to be an individual human being is now an intellectual monster. There is no longer "a person", but a **member** of a race, a gender, a religion, an ethnic group, an economic group, a political faction. When alone, or in a dream state, the person might think independently a bit, but in the presence of other people the collectivist mentality takes control, and quite literally controls the person's life, his view of reality and those of his conclusions that are important to the group. (Prof. Irving Janis, of Yale University, coined the term "group-think", while another source said it was William Whyte, Jr., of Fortune

Magazine.) The person polices his own thoughts in terror of being ostracized by his in-group. To be perfectly clear, the positions of the "in-group" will be held **though they are obviously lies.** Parents who aren't getting along to begin with, fight viciously over who gets to "brainwash" the children, with the less rational parent always fighting the hardest, and dirtiest, (recall the Bible story of the two women who approached the king, each claiming the same child as her own.) And almost everyone is a collectivist to some degree, and almost everyone thinks they are not to any degree.

When the errors of a persons' "in-group" eventually loom too large, (i.e., affects **him** too negatively), he will occasionally leave the group, but almost always to the other side, regardless of **that** sides' errors. (see "Polarization", page 100. Just a few of the more famous "switches" in the **political field** have been Whittaker Chambers, Paul Crouch, David Horowitz, and to a lesser extent, Christopher Hitchens.) The important thing is to feel safe – safe from aloneness, safe from other groups, safe from uncertainty, safe from one's own limited rationality. The real purpose of identifying one's personality with such interest groups is the opportunities afforded to **use others** and get away with it, or to **play a role of victim with the group** --whichever is more expedient in the moment. Independent men will be singled out by groups for persecution **simply for the sin of being independent!** Men who are the targets of such campaigns can find their options of life severely limited. For example, during slavery, and afterwards, "Jim Crow", whites who disagreed suffered real consequences for their principles – an often overlooked or minimized fact in popular accounts of equal rights struggles. Even today, independent men with better ideas remain ostracized. These are some reasons why men over-identify with interest groups and the reason why they remain so.

When one has the collectivist mentality, of what use is Intellectual Curiosity (other than one's job, or hobbies)? – useless. Of what use is Intellectual Honesty? -- it is sensed as the gravest of dangers. But no one sees themselves this way! And fish don't have a word for "water". **So intellectual independency/ dependency seem the greatest of the virtues and vices.**

100 SCIENTISTS WROTE A PAPER ON WHY MY THEORY IS WRONG.
IF MY THEORY WAS WRONG ONE SCIENTIST
WOULD HAVE BEEN ENOUGH.
Albert Einstein

I will give a personal example of the insidious nature of collectivism which illustrates the generality of the problem. I was raised in a home that was not very collectivist minded. Also, my local culture was quite **religiously homogenous** – in other words, the local culture, as a whole, was about as collectivist as any other, yet there was little conflict or friction with other competing religious groups. As the result of these conditions the "group" was simply taken for granted, culturally, and little dwelled upon. Therefore, due to my upbringing and these conditions the word "nation" was for me equal to and completely interchangeable with the word "country" – to me they were exactly the same thing -- a total redundancy. It wasn't until I was well into my adulthood that I encountered **that other** use of the word "nation" – the **ethnic** usage! Eventually I came to realize that, when spoken by certain people, the phrase "one nation", in the Pledge of Allegiance, promised quite the opposite of unity for our country. I was, and still am, intellectually appalled that anyone would consider themselves a member of any group other than **the citizens of a free country.**

Living in what has been one of the freest places on Earth (i.e., more rational than has been typical for man), the people of the United States have little understanding of the insidious nature and great danger of collectivism – to them it is merely a game they are playing to get their way. Stripped of collectivism, the other Vices of intellectual dullness and dishonesty are only so much stupidity and crime. But collectivism **institutionalizes stupidity and legalizes crime against the individual**! Collectivism is the "gateway drug" to the stupidity of Intellectual Dullness and the violence of Intellectual Dishonesty. It is only a matter of time which group finally gets control. The American people do not understand,,,,,, but they are about to. The single greatest obstacle to the salvation of mankind has been his refusal to give up his collectivism and live as individuals.

So, in a sense, the challenge for men is the prospect of "re-parenting" themselves, as adults, in the sense of re-considering all the ideas and notions which they absorbed unquestioningly as children. In our volitional view of man there is a tension between holding him responsible for the way he is while being mindful of his previous life as an innocent and helpless child.

One may now clearly see why I set out at once to keep my final conclusions in this Book to a minimum. Rational thinking means conforming to the facts of the world in which we live. There are correct conclusions, but one can only reason one's way to them by one's own effort; otherwise one is at the mercy of every hack, crook or charlatan that comes along, especially politicians. I am telling you the truth, not what to think. I know that you think you are clever, but I promise you there are bad people more clever than you, and they are running your life – they are tricking you with your own fears and desires.

When I reflect on the general state of man's rationality I sometimes truly wonder how man ever crawled out from his caves, yet still fights and harms one another. But I answer my own questions – I am showing exactly how man has achieved such marvelous feats of material progress yet still does not live in harmony.

> IT IS NOT TRUTH THAT MAKES MAN GREAT,
> BUT MAN THAT MAKES TRUTH GREAT.
>> Confucius

> PEOPLE WILL FORGIVE YOU FOR BEING WRONG,
> BUT NOT FOR BEING RIGHT.
>> Peter Kreeft

VIRTUE IS GUARANTEE OF RATIONALITY

The Primary Virtues describe the totality of a man's volitional thinking – they are the three aspects of rationality. When practiced **properly** and **consistently** then a man is rational. If a man turns out not to be rational it is because he missed a step along his way. To achieve rationality the virtues must be actually be practiced – simply telling oneself that one is doing it won't do.

In pop-psychology much is made of ideas such as "self esteem", "finding oneself", "finding one's purpose", "the meaning of life", "mindfulness", etc. The answer to all these things, and much more, is **rationality.** How can one have these things without the virtues of Intellectual Independence, Intellectual Curiosity, and Intellectual Honesty? A man cannot. But, practicing them, these things are possible.

> TO PROCEED FROM THE KNOWLEDGE OF BOOKS
> TO THE KNOWLEDGE OF LIFE,
> MERE THINKING IS NOT ENOUGH.
>> Lin Yutang
>> The Importance Of Living

THE SYNERGY OF THE VIRTUES

The term "synergy" has been around for a while. It's meaning is: The whole being more, or better, than the simple sum of its parts. To the extent that a man practices the Primary Virtues, he will be rational; and to the extent that a man is rational he will be patient, kind, intelligent, just, curious, prepared, flexible yet principled, insightful, industrious, efficient, wise, humorous, hopeful (to the extent possible), romantic and affectionate, honest, grateful and genuine – in other words, the man will be **well rounded.** It is not in my writing of this that makes it so – it has always been the case that it is the practice of the Virtues that makes a man effective. In trying to improve oneself, or one's relations with others, it is the Virtues that will do it. The Virtues are how a man **finds peace with himself.**

> I WAS ASHAMED WHEN I REALIZED THAT LIFE WAS A COSTUME PARTY
> AND I ATTENDED WITH MY REAL FACE.
> Franz Kafka

THE NON-CONCEPTUAL MENTALITY

On the other hand, the practice of the Primary Vices guarantees a different mental state – the irrational non-conceptual mentality. In this mentality the skill of **properly** stacking and cross referencing high level concepts is undeveloped. The events of life seem only vaguely connected, at least until it is too late. Life is lived according to a set of rules which cannot be practiced consistently, i.e., one doesn't simply make mistakes, but rather "is a sinner". One might be extremely intelligent in one or more particular subjects, yet the knowledge remains dis-articulated from one's concept structure and of less use in other important areas of life.

> THERE IS ALWAYS PLENTY OF LIFE TO ENJOY FOR A MAN DETERMINED TO ENJOY IT.
> IF MEN FAIL TO ENJOY THIS EARTHLY EXISTENCE IT IS BECAUSE THEY
> DO NOT LOVE LIFE SUFFICIENTLY AND ALLOW IT TO BE TURNED INTO
> A HUMDRUM ROUTINE EXISTENCE.
> Lin Yutang
> The Importance Of Living

PAIN

Further, the practice of the Vices guarantees another mental state -- PAIN. To the extent that a man is intellectually dependent he will experience self-doubt and self-alienation; to the extent that a man is intellectually dull or lazy he will be bored, confused and un-knowing; and to the extent that he practices intellectual dishonesty he will feel guilty and un-deserving of happiness.

Although men must deal with a world filled largely with irrational others, which at times can be quite difficult, it is often the practice of a man's own vices which contribute to personal problems such as anger, impatience, addictions and phobias, poor sleep, lifestyle-caused poor health, and general relationship problems.

43

COMPARTMENTALIZATION

A very common situation is to find a person who is obviously bright in one or more fields, often some technical, mechanical, or career area, yet who clearly has difficulties in other important areas of life. This is because Intellectual Curiosity is the easiest Virtue to "lean on" while allowing the others to languish. Intellectual Curiosity deals with nature and existence itself, and nature is **un-compromising and un-manipulative.** When one goes out into the world one must express a certain amount of rationality, or fail. But as one gets closer to dealing with others, or with oneself, Intellectual Dependency and Intellectual Dishonesty kick in. So with compartmentalization we see bright professional people with messed up lives, messed up relationships, messed up kids, messed up views on government and social issues. It is not because dealing with oneself or others is particularly complex, but rather that the other Primary Virtues are less operative.

Furthermore, the world in which we live is **designed by, and for, irrational people.** A man lives an unavoidably social existence with other **irrational** men. Even a well-rounded rational man of the Primary Virtues fights a never-ending battle with the irrational men around him. When one finds a person who "doesn't fit in", it is usually that he is less rational than the average man, but not always.

This concept of compartmentalization elegantly explains why man has made such great progress in his factual knowledge, technology and material comforts, while the **humanities are in shambles** – man's ethical and political progress is a failure. Compartmentalized thinking plays a large role the mechanistic (i.e., non-volitional) view of man discussed previously. It is practiced by even the most intelligent and respected authorities of society. It explains why men who fancy themselves "intellectuals" are overwhelmingly found on the political Left. The phenomenon has been observed through the ages. For example, Aristotle talks of two kinds of knowledge; the "techne", from which our word "technology" comes, and the "Sophia", his word for "wisdom". As go the societies' individuals, so goes the society.

One fine example of compartmentalized thinking was the writer George Orwell, who wrote well known books (correctly) condemning Totalitarianism, yet who considered himself a "Democratic Socialist" – a **massive contradiction in**

thought. It makes no moral difference whether the "many are persecuted by the few" (al dictatorships), or the "few by the many" (al Democratic Socialism). In fact, if anything, it is the persecution of the "few by the many" of socialism that is **more** morally reprehensible! The maintenance of a societies' cultural, ethical and political values requires the practice of all of the Primary Virtues by a critical fraction of citizens.

(The fact that <u>Nineteen Eighty-Four</u> was written by an avowed Democratic Socialist is interesting psychologically and politically. It is why the work is touted in the West as the "go to" dystopian novel, while an available better alternative is not. In my copy of the work the Afterward was even written by Erich Fromm, another Democratic Socialist. None of this is mere coincidence. The subtle message intended to be conveyed is that while totalitarianism communism is not compatible with freedom, socialism somehow is.)

> THE SADDEST ASPECT OF LIFE RIGHT NOW
> IS THAT SCIENCE GATHERS KNOWLEDGE
> FASTER THAN SOCIETY GATHERS WISDOM.
> Isaac Asimov

This is an excellent place to mention one of my pet peeves. It is the portrayal in everyday society, and in particular the media, of men being more rational than they are, i.e., more intellectually independent, curious, and honest than people are in real life. There are sound **artistic** reasons for this, but in mass society that is usually not the case. I am fully aware that, as things stand now, it would be impossible to have general social interactions, or any advertising or entertainment industry without putting up some kind of "front". This is merely to point out that there are different reasons for the idealized portrayal of human character traits, and they are not all of equal value. Still, such ubiquitous idealizations do give the false impression that rationality is an effortless matter of course, and encourage and facilitate a vicariously lived false rationality. It is part of the problem of collectivism, and a subtle form of flattery of their audience when done by the media. The "pitches" are generally very slick. I recall one clever drama series called "Brothers And Sisters", featuring Sally Field. All problems were solved by the end of each hour, thereby restoring "wonderful". But you just can't beat the current vicarious drama series, literally called "This Is

45

Us". There is a little something for everyone in this show – one episode even portrayed a menage-a-trois, (not that I'm against menage-a-trois).

It is well understood that men frequently live vicariously through various aspects of their surroundings, but little thought is given that this extends to their most fundamental character traits as well. Western culture as a whole was, until several generations ago, the most rational that the world had ever known, but as that culture now falls apart this "putting up a front" becomes glaringly absurd to the rational man.

THE BABY AND THE BATH WATER

The conceptual mentality is a "system builder", able to study perceived things **in their parts**. The world being as it is, there are normally both true and false ideas to be discerned. Even if all the ideas that one happened upon were true, it would still be necessary to validate each on its own terms. Therefore, the conceptual mentality is not particularly troubled that ideas from any source are often a mix of true and false. Rather, the question that the rational man asks himself is, "is there likely to be enough of value in this material to devote my time and pleasure to it?".

But, once again, the non-conceptual mentality is in a different position. In the non-conceptual man **perception is his attempted means of thinking.** The non-conceptual man "swallows things whole". He wants a whole book, or ready-made way of life, to which he can subscribe. False ideas are glossed over, or else held to be true. He considers himself not responsible for the way things are. Though he will acknowledge that "no one is perfect", the really big problems in life are not caused by his approach, he thinks, but by others'. In contrast to the rational man, when the irrational man is presented with new material, his operative thought is, "with what in here do I agree, or disagree?". For the irrational man, perception is his means of knowing -- his conceptual faculty is undeveloped – it comes down to whom he chooses to believe.

> NO MAN IS SO BLIND AS HE WHO REFUSES TO SEE.
> Unknown

Poor idea-discrimination skills in men present a **great danger** when it comes to learning from men who purport to teach, or following men who aspire to lead. The problem is that the more polished are the ideas presented by a teacher

46

or leader, the **more difficult are their errors to detect.** It is tempting to simply believe and follow men who sound so good. But if what a man wants is to think correctly, then a "little error" is like a "little cancer" – the small error introduces contradictions between a man's intentions, his actions and their results. Sooner or later, in future generations perhaps, the little error has become a monster. Social Security, for example, or any government "welfare program" ever conceived – all are now devastating failures, yet all sounded so "reasonable" and "necessary" when instituted. It is a fact that the more correct a thinker is, the more dangerous he is! One thing I learn from writing is that one can say almost anything one wants to say, provided he can figure out how to say it! The reader should keep mindful of this when encountering ideas that sound good.

But I am being too generous even in the above examples. Take Social Security for instance. When the program was instituted males were the primary work-force on record, yet few men lived long enough to receive much of their contribution. Therefore, **even on its face**, the program was a **forced** transfer of property from **men to their widows,** and the society wanted this. But it is actually even worse than that! – a moment's reflection will show that the attack was **doubly upon bachelors** who would have no widows to benefit!

(The Supreme Court had threatened to block Social Security. The **American People,** in response, threatened to pack the Court if it did not allow as constitutional what everyone knew was not constitutional. The pressure was, and has always been, for the Court to permit any **programs and expenditures** enacted by Congress – which it has essentially done. As far as its Constitutional duties were concerned, the Court was left with little choice but to content itself with "protecting the citizen's rights". The American people are about to see how that turned out.)

A HALF TRUTH IS MORE DANGEROUS THAN A COMPLETE LIE.
St. Thomas Aquinas

There is another tragic aspect to a man getting his philosophy "almost right" rather than "right". As a set of principles are lived, sooner or later any contradictions built into that philosophy will come to light. Such a state of affairs might happen quickly during the lifetime of a single person, or it could take generations, as in the progression of a country. This second tragic aspect is that the vast majority of men observe this failure **and conclude that a right philosophy is not possible** – that no man could possibly understand life

47

adequately to prevent personal or social catastrophe – and so men simply give up. "After all", they think, "if the smartest people in the world cannot really understand life, then what hope is there?". Obviously, I would not be writing this Book if I believed that that were true.

EMOTIONS – A CASE STUDY

> WE WHO WILL DIE ARE THE LUCKY ONES,
> FOR THERE ARE THOSE WHO WILL NEVER DIE
> BECAUSE THEY NEVER LIVED.
> Richard Dawkins

We are now in position to discuss a notable emotion in some detail, shedding additional light on emotions' general role in cognition.

Recall the overall perspectives from which we viewed emotions – how something is **interpreted as** either "good for you" or "bad for you"; that the emotion is regarding something "about you" or "about your surroundings"; and that the emotion is either a direct motivator or reward/warning.

Now consider the following emotion: The brain perceives something outside of itself which, in itself, would not evoke much emotion. Within this perception the brain detects a reflection of one of its own ideas, concepts, positions or general impressions. A stronger emotion than expected, called **satisfaction,** is produced. To illustrate the point and drive it home I will make up an extreme example. Suppose Isaac Newton has just spent the Summer discovering calculus to demonstrate his theories of mechanics (a profound satisfaction in itself, and not too far from what actually happened). Then, at the same time, another man (Leibniz), in another place, was also discovering calculus (again, not too far from what actually happened). Though the two men may have never met, they certainly could have, and they presumably became aware of each other's work. Setting aside the possible rivalry aspect of the matter, as well as each man's **separate** esthetic response, the feeling of satisfaction in each man, aware of his work in the other, may have been significant. All of this emotion is called the **Esthetic Response**, or simply "Esthetics".

Running the emotion through our "emotion analyzer", we see that the emotion is "positive", and though it is triggered by an outward perception it is **in response to something inside the man,** and it is a "reward". The emotion caused

48

by the response says, "I am right", "I am rational", "I am capable of living", etc. Since a man can make errors in all aspects of his thinking, the emotion can be "true" or "false". If the object of perception conforms to the facts of reality and the emotion is positive, then the emotion is "true". If the observer is (on that particular issue) in error, and the object perceived or his response do not conform to reality, then the emotion is false and will be a further, and possibly powerful, source of deception and confusion for the man.

The rational man loves nature and loves conforming to it, so nature does provide him with some opportunities for esthetic response. Such opportunities tend, however, to be rather abstract: beautiful sunsets, beautiful animals, a noble pet dog, forests, mountains, fresh air, the first cool puff of fall breeze after a sweltering southern summer, or perhaps, (not as abstract) viewing a total eclipse of the sun. (I cried upon seeing my first one, a bit unexpectedly. But I'm just a cold engineer with all those science and math courses behind me, and all of the books I've been reading these years, so I had only a fuzzy idea of what I was witnessing – it just "looked pretty".)

But as esthetically pleasing as nature is to the rational man, he wants even more. Recall that the brain has the capacity to treat concepts as if they were percepts, and so the brain also has the ability to "see" concepts that are embedded within percepts. So the rational man wants to be surrounded by "beautiful" **man-made** things that evoke his positive esthetic response – he builds beautiful buildings and houses, gardens and yards, attractive cities and streets, he keeps himself and his surroundings relatively clean, he wants to live under a proper government in a society where men are benevolent and honor each other's rights, he wants meaningful friendships, family, and a very close relationship, or two, that mostly share his ideas, he has meaningful pass times and leisure activities. Certain people are moved to create things with little material purpose, but rather to share their ideas and view of life with others in the attempt to elicit their esthetic response – books, music, paintings, sculpture, poetry, movies, religious symbols and icons, a national flag, a national anthem, etc., -- these are all man-made things created either to elicit the esthetic response, or sought after to evoke the response. However, it cannot be overemphasized that a man's ideas can be "true" or "false". The experience of a positive esthetic response does not mean that a man is "correct" on an issue, but only that he **agrees with the perception in question.**

The rational man wants to be educated so as to enjoy all these things to a reasonable extent. He is a good role model for others and his children. The sum of all these activities, and much, much more, is a man's "culture".

We have described the esthetic life of the rational man, but the irrational man leads a different kind of existence. The irrational man conforms to nature when expedient in the moment. When not expedient he attempts to bend nature to his desires, which often involves harming others in some way, for example: the slave holder, or the "tax and spend" voter. Rather than having beautiful things that embody his ideas, he "keeps up appearances". Perhaps very tellingly, some irrational men have a tendency to be hyper-interested in certain works of art, (paintings, fiction literature, etc.), since reality may not provide him with adequate esthetic response, and might even threaten his ideas. The irrational man needs man-made art to "tell his story". He may seek to force his art into the public square.

To further contrast the two approaches – for the rational man, the esthetic response provides "satisfaction" or "fulfillment", while the irrational man seeks **"validation"**. The irrational man corrupts his cognition by attempting to experience his esthetics as **motivator emotions** when they are designed to be a **reward.** And finally, for the rational man the esthetic response is more of a **serendipitous event,** while the irrational man will more often actively seek the experience, i.e., he is "motivated".

Some men are moved to produce somber works of art (primarily literature) in the attempt to elicit an esthetic **warning** response. Books like <u>Animal Farm</u>, <u>Nineteen Eighty-Four</u>, and <u>Atlas Shrugged</u>, foresaw the end results of irrational ethics and politics, (Politics to be detailed in the following Part). The late 1960's, 70's, and early 80's were a time of hope for our society, and such was expressed in some good popular music. But there were songs intended to elicit warning as well -- just a few of many possible examples that come to mind include "Hotel California", Jackson Browne's "Boulevard", and The Who's "Won't Get Fooled Again". A English play, also made into a movie, was The Rocky Horror Show -- another story of warning . The rational man responds deeply and appropriately to such works, while the irrational man cannot respond adequately. Witness the albeit modest sensation experienced by <u>Atlas Shrugged </u>(a 50 year-old book) after the first "Bush Bailout" in the late 2000's. Yet today, as conditions are much deteriorated since then, little is heard of the breathtaking work. In reality, the interest spike was primarily caused by some conservatives consuming the story for **validation** -- most readers simply **projecting onto** the work their own limited understanding of ethics and politics. Now the book is passe', its entertainment value used up like an old rag time songs'. Though the work is now 60 sum years old, it is said to still sell many thousands of copies a year. Clearly, too few of these new readers really "get" the message, for if freedom were receiving this many new spokesmen (and voters) per year, the society could not be in the shape it now is. But for the rational man, good art never dies. There are people read "Atlas" numerous times during their lives,,,,,,,,,, and it is a big book!

I wish to emphasize that the **quality** of the esthetic response is dependent on the **richness** of a man's understanding of, and relation to, reality – mere intelligence does not do it. What is commonly understood as "intelligence" is only an **aspect** of the Virtue of Intellectual Curiosity. Some very intelligent men live quite empty lives. The irrational man still wants to have a fulfilling life and senses that something is missing. To the extent that his ideas and conclusions are false and contradictory he cannot experience esthetic fulfillment, so he attempts to **fake it** with made up goals and standards which can be met **without exercise of the Primary Virtues** – he thereby feels validation and calls it fulfillment. He attempts to evoke the esthetic response **without enacting its cause,** since his thinking is circular. He cannot believe that another man without his made up goals and standards can have his experience, when, in fact, the rational man's experience is superior and yields actual satisfaction and fulfillment. Contrast this with a simple man (though he may be less formally educated) with a fuller relationship to the world around him – such a man might live an esthetically fulfilling life, at least regarding the aspects of his life independent of the problems of other men.

This topic explains why man-made art and fiction have only limited potential to effect lasting positive change, as it is not generally pursued with change as a priority! -- the irrational man is primarily seeking entertainment and validation, while the rational man is seeking to rest and enjoy his achievements.

Finally, I point out the highest opportunity for experiencing one's own rationality in the esthetic response, and so too the one with the highest stakes – rearing children. Need I point out the prevalence of people having children not for fulfillment but for self-validation?

COMPASSION / BENEVOLENCE / JUSTICE / EQUALITY / ETC.

Simple consideration shows that admirable emotions and concepts such as compassion, benevolence, justice and equality, and others that men have towards man and other living things arise out of the esthetic response. All these are ideas that have naturally occurred to men throughout the ages, and can occur again. A man sees in other men, and in living things, reflections of himself. Since the rational man is imminently good to himself he wants to be surrounded by good treatment of other beings. Since the rational man is beautiful on the inside he wants to be surrounded by beautiful things on the outside, including beautiful lives of others. He sees that poor treatment of other beings, if accepted, could readily become poor treatment of himself. Beware the man who says he is doing something "only for you" – he is surely doing it only for himself.

The esthetic response is a very old "feedback", or "positive reinforcement" mechanism for the furtherance of man's survival, to encourage him to learn from his environment. The response evolved having nothing to do with man's enjoyment of man-made art or other aspects of modern society. The production and enjoyment of such things is only a **resultant** of man's esthetic response and his intelligence. In our view of life, "morality" is a **form of knowledge** man gains by self-reflection in relation to his surroundings, and not mere opinion or a set of instructions that man receives from on high.

In the natural environment a man can trust his esthetic responses. To use simple examples, if a man sees a beautiful sunset, and has a positive response, he can believe that his emotion is "true". To continue, if a man sees his friend attacked by a lion, or his own pet dies, he can again trust his negative esthetic responses. However, with men's volition also come men's errors and evil. When it comes to perception of the man-made he can no longer automatically trust his esthetic responses. For example: a government official comes along, elicits sympathy for children of parents in poverty, and proposes a government solution to the problem. In such a case a highly rational man will have one esthetic response toward the unfortunate child victims, another regarding the mothers who choose to produce children though unable to secure their care, and still another for the politician who proposes to make it easier, nay profitable!, to engage in such behavior with a government program for which citizens are forced to pay – **and know exactly why he reacts as he does**.

MOTIVATING RATIONALITY

I have discussed how the esthetic response is one of the rational man's rewards for living, and how the irrational man has a disordered relationship to the emotion. But, also as previously discussed, thinking requires a motivating emotion as well. Therefore, what is the **motivating emotion** for the whole of a man's rationality? – it is the emotion of **pride.** Pride is why the rational man thinks independently; it is why he is intellectually curious; and it is why he is intellectually honest. The rational man is his own best critic. He remembers his mistakes as well, or better than his successes. His conclusions, though they may be well thought out, remain open to question and change because he wants to be **correct,** not "right" in the eyes of himself or others. He is "open minded" in the best sense of that concept. The rational man doesn't think in terms of "good enough", but in terms of "good". He is motivated by the sense of pride.

And again, just as with the esthetic response, the irrational man has a disordered relationship with the emotion of pride. He reverses cause and effect by attempting to experience pride as a reward, rather than its intended motivating function.

So, finally, this begs the question of what is a man's **reward emotion** for the whole of his rationality? The reader already knows the term – it is **self-esteem!**

ANOTHER NOTABLE MOTIVATOR EMOTION

Just to show that not all negative **de-motivator** emotions are bad, we present **Guilt,** and **the Conscience.**

But first we must dispense with a false or useless guilt we shall call "social guilt". This is the emotion one has when either contemplating, or actually acting contrary to the dictates of one's "in-group" (which can just as easily be a single person). The in-group, or "in-person", has trained the subject (via. his intellectual dependence) that this feeling is guilt when it is actually fear – fear of the group. You get that? The group has brain-washed, and the subject accepted, the switching of guilt (actually fear of the group) in exchange for self-loathing! The contemplated action evoking the emotion **may in fact be a bad thing to do.** The problem is that the irrational man has no way of independently verifying whether the act is evil or good. **To the extent that the subject is irrational** he is as lost with as without the social guilt. The hilarious thing is that this guilt is quite tolerable – it is like a "cost of doing business". One just does whatever one really wants to do, and then pays for it with an adequate amount of "guilt" (self-loathing) to the group.

In speaking of social guilt we are not primarily thinking about objective laws against killing, stealing, pollution, etc. – rather, we are talking about the improper government regulation and control, victimless crime laws, and all the little ways that men want to micro-manage the lives of others.

Is social guilt necessary? It is woven into the irrational fabric of society and just as much evil is committed with it as without it. Social guilt has little power to control behavior or make men good, as people implicitly know that arbitrary rules devised by other people for their own convenience do not have authority. Besides, as soon as no one is looking the actions proscribed by social guilt are readily undertaken. It would be nice if all social expectation and shaming were rational, objective – but such has never been, nor likely will ever be the case. The tragic thing for the individual is that so many people remain stuck in social guilt and never experience the real thing – what we shall call **metaphysical guilt!** In this segue we note that social guilt is the emoting regarding **one's surroundings**, as the higher animals do, while metaphysical guilt is the **emoting regarding oneself** (in relation to one's surroundings) – the distinctly human characteristic!

Unlike social guilt, metaphysical guilt is painful and intolerable to the rational man, causing a genuine hesitancy to act. Running the emotion through our emotion analyzer, we see that the emotion is negative (something is bad for you), it is about something "in you", and it is a "de-motivator" emotion. The emotion is a **signal** from the brain that it is being asked to hold a contradiction – i.e., a disconnect between reality and what the subject wants to conclude.

Previously we had theorized that once the brain arrives at the higher conceptual stage the volition steps in to give the brain conceptual "options" to consider. We also theorized that the **mind** could at that point **direct** the brain as to which option to accept as the best. But the mind makes mistakes, and apparently the brain has a built-in aversion to contradictions. We know that this might be true since first level concepts are built by the brain almost automatically and flawlessly. The brain knows how to group "like things", and there is no reason to suppose that it can't group "like concepts" as well. So it seems that the brain might have the ability to "catch up" with the mind, and send it a signal that a mistake has been made – metaphysical guilt. Again, a misconception might be that metaphysical guilt comes from some "social conscience", when this is not the case – it comes from the facts of reality.

Now we can see **degrees of evil.** The first stage, when the mistake has been made but before the brain has registered the error. The second stage, when the mistake has registered and the guilt signal sent, but then **ignored.** And the third, and final stage, when the guilt signals have been **repressed.** In the final stage the subject fully thinks that he is acting virtuously and correctly – and he will act unhesitatingly and guiltlessly. Note that the person in stage three evil remains just as culpable, though he is unaware of it. As the saying goes, the road to hell is paved with good intentions ,,,,,,,,,, so it is.

It is important to make a point, clarifying the preceding paragraph. The relationship of guilt to evil described above is a **private matter** for the man himself. A man's ideas and conclusions are his alone and a man cannot be judged until he **acts,** for to do otherwise would require mind reading. However, once a man acts he may then, and should, be judged. If on any issue his actions are consistent with reality and promote human wellbeing (in the long range), then, on that particular issue, we may assume that the man is rational (good). If the man's actions **occasionally** conflict with reality and are a detriment to human well-being (in the long range), but with results which are not excessively harmful, then we may assume that the man might be trying to reason, yet be making honest errors. If, on the other hand, the man consistently takes actions detrimental to human life, or commits isolated acts of serious harm, then we may judge him as evil to some degree. Obviously, if a man consistently makes good judgements in his conclusions and actions, then he should be judged as a rational (good) man, even though he will make mistakes. A man's actions include everything he does, including the writing of books or doing speaking engagements to promote his ideas, as well as voting in elections for candidates of his choice – these too are actions to be judged.

When a man speaks, too, he is acting. If logical gibberish issues forth from his mouth we may assume that he is intellectually dull. If he is comfortable in his dullness we may assume it is because he is intellectually dishonest. If he is comfortable in his intellectual dishonesty it is because he can get away with it. And if he can get away with it, it is because he is intellectually dependent upon an in-group which tells him he is right and defends him from outsiders who might attempt to set him straight in his thinking.

Finally, one particular class of men deserving special scrutiny are those who put themselves forward as intellectuals and then promulgate their ideas, as I am doing right now.

Upon experiencing the conflicts between reality and their early-acquired concepts, usually at a young age, a few individuals will become rational, but most will repress and end up as irrational. In adults one is rarely observing the **process** but rather **only the end result**. Usually, only in children can one observe the ongoing process of achieving rationality or repression – and then only by paying very close attention.

As one example of the intellectual torture children are subjected to, I offer the following: In the year 2020, in the United States, a class of high school students are compelled to watch a presidential debate, and then write an essay on it. The assignment is wrong, very wrong, on at least the following points:

1) No person should ever be told **what** to write about unless they are, **a)** a professional writer in the employ of a concern, or **b)** a student in some elective course. Writing, unique to humans, is a creative endeavor of the highest order. To tell a young student what to write about, who not only may have no interest in writing, but also little or no interest or knowledge of what he is being compelled to write about, essentially treats the activity like so much grammar, punctuation and sentence structure – which it is not. Introducing students to the skill of writing may indeed be a fine thing, but killing any desire to write by forcing them to write on matters of which they may have little or no interest or knowledge seems counter-productive. Perhaps more to the point, the school assignment reflects a **false concept of creativity** – that man simply creates something from nothing, which is not how it works. (One obvious exception to the above would be simple essay answers on student tests which are indeed a good thing.)

2) Here in the West we so take our freedoms for granted and are **throwing them away**. Having a child write a political paper, in a government school, and then be judged on it is to be expected in places such as the totalitarian Soviet Union, Germany, China, North Korea, or any other dictatorship – but not in a free society. Having children expose the political affiliation of themselves, and hence their families, in a government school, to teachers and administrators employed by that government, is highly inappropriate! The next logical step in this practice would be , of course, to have the students write at school in the presence of their overseers rather than at home with their parents -- if this hasn't already happened somewhere!

3) The "debates" are not debates at all but an irrational hash of smears, lies and vote-buying promises. Once again we see the false concept of creativity which implies that man simply creates something from nothing -- and the debates **are nothing.** Forcing students to make any kind of sense of this tripe, as if it meant anything, is worse than evil, if that is possible.

I have covered what I have termed the Primary Virtues and Vices. In reality each of them is associated with any number of derivative practices required to live an effective or ineffective life, whichever one so chooses. For example, the practice of Intellectual Honesty requires the stand that one support oneself by one's own thought and effort, that one be honest both in thought and action, that one consider all relevant facts to an issue, that one refrain from conclusions not warranted by sufficient knowledge, that one has cause to think that he **has** sufficient knowledge, etc. Likewise, the other Primary Virtues of Independence and Curiosity have derivative virtues and stands needed by the individual to function rationally.

THE METAPHYSICALLY GIVEN AND THE MAN-MADE

> So things stood in the years after Einstein arrived in the patent office in 1902. In his patent work he had, in the instructions given by (his supervisor), the directive to be critical at every stage: "When you pick up an application, think that anything the inventor says is wrong." To follow blindly would be to court disaster by following "the inventors way of thinking, and that will prejudice you. You have to remain critically vigilant."
>
> ESSAY: Einstein's Clocks: The Place Of Time
> Peter Galison

We now cover an important concept regarding correct thinking, and one that is widely violated. In Metaphysics it was stated that existence must be accepted without question – it just is! This was not intended to imply that man then sits and does nothing. Man certainly acts upon nature as he should and must. The point now being made is the **distinction** between "nature" and "man's acting on nature". In nature everything is perfect and happens as it should. Storms, earthquakes, disease, various accidents, death – these things are not to be judged – they just are. Man is not victimized by nature --- man is victimized by MEN! It is the man-made that is to be judged. In fact, everything that man does must be judged! All of man's institutions, all his governments, all of his rules and laws, customs, habits, etc., must past the tests of Ethics and Politics. This is the rational man's approach. The fact that things might have been done a certain way in the past does not necessarily mean that they were right for then, or for now. (We are reminded here of the philosophical Maxim of, "the burden of proof is on he who asserts the positive", (Page 21), where all of man's actions and creations are, in fact, "positives to be proven".)

But the irrational man has a different approach. He either judges nature (the things he doesn't want to accept) or declares man-made things to be beyond question (the things he wants to impose onto others!) – he generally does this by declaring those particular things are not man-made when they really are . What then ensues in society is a "war of the hypocrites". Certainly the most famous words ever spoken regarding the metaphysically given vs. the man-made were by Francis Bacon – "Nature to be commanded, must be obeyed." Such is the motto of the rational man.

> I WOULD RATHER HAVE QUESTIONS
> THAT CAN'T BE ANSWERED
> THAN ANSWERS THAT
> CAN'T BE QUESTIONED.
>
> Richard Feynman

We have described in Ethics the three fundamental problems that all men must face, and the ineffective and effective mental states for dealing with them. All men answer these challenges in their own varying ways and degrees of

58

success.   It is these unique responses among men that give them their **personalities**, yet the fundamental problems faced were all the same.   Stripped of the personality we are simply left with the degree of a man's rationality, i.e., his virtues and vices.

Psychologists study personality and devise theories, hoping to explain, predict and help people improve their lives. This is all well and good, yet it is important to be mindful that personality is not man's most fundamental quality – it is his virtues and vices.   Also, common parlance holds that it is their personalities that makes men unique. However, this is little more than a truism, not much more than the statement that "No two snowflakes are alike." It is what lies beneath the personality, the degree of men's rationality, that truly sets them apart from one another, and what really matters.

I will close this Part with some ethical problems for the reader himself to consider in relation to the Primary Virtues and Vices. However, I will outline a couple of notable ones in some detail to illustrate the process. Consider, for example, the issue of **"stress"**. Stress is the condition of having an insufficient "tool box" of concepts to meet present demands of circumstances – one feels "overwhelmed". Better conceptual thinking helps one avoid the feeling of stress. Non-conceptual thinkers can be very subject to stress – they are easily overwhelmed by the particulars of life. People can cause stress by going along with their "in-group" in doing activities for which they are unsuited. They can attempt to fulfill unrealistic obligations expected by their in-group or person in their life (intellectual dependency). One can cause their own stress by "taking on too much", a form of intellectual dishonesty. One can think of other ways in which living the Primary Virtues will help one with the issue of stress.

This is not to automatically disparage various techniques that might be available to reduce stress when there might be no advantage to feeling it. But such techniques are similar to using drugs to help people through difficult times. The goal should be to treat the cause and not simply the symptom. Stress is a warning emotion that something is not right. I promised in this Book to be solution oriented rather than problem oriented. The cure for stress is not simply to attempt to stop feeling it, but to adjust one's approach to life activities and developing better thinking skills.

Closely related to the non-conceptual mentality and stress seems to be the issue of **"control"**. If a man feels easily overwhelmed he may be tempted to over-control his surroundings, or even himself, and in particular those pesky unpredictable people around him. In advanced cases the "control freak" might attempt to control simply for the sake of staying in practice. The control can become a habit – an addiction. The stressed person feels that the **attempted elimination of surprises** will help reduce his stress, when in fact it further adds to his problems.

So think about how practicing the Primary Virtues or Vices might relate to the following sample of issues:

What causes addiction? Are you easily bored? Might these be related?
Might other forms of intellectual pain contribute to addiction?
What is "brainwashing"? Can a grown rational adult really be brainwashed?
Why would a person want to alter their mind with drugs?
Why is the society hooked on caffeine?
What is a "need based life", vs. a "want based life"? Which would be happier?
Do you find many people who understand you, or few?
Do you find this book's individual-centered viewpoint of life to be cynical?
Why has man's greatly increased leisure not helped him, but harmed him?

SUMMARY OF ETHICS

1) Ethics is the study of the proper rules to guide man's life as an individual.

2) Man's life is but a series of highly varied problems to be solved, however, man's problems begin as intellectual.

3) Man's problems are in response to his existence in the real world.

4) When life is conceptualized down to its fundamentals, there are only three existents with which men must deal. They are:
   a) The minds of other men
   b) The whole of nature and his physical existence, including the motives and actions of other men
   c) His own mind

5) The three fundamental problems faced by all men are the failure to deal with the three fundamental existents. They are:
   a) Intellectual Dependency – the failure to sufficiently distance his mind from the minds of others
   b) Intellectual Dullness/Laziness – the failure to adequately understand the world in which he lives, including the motives and actions of other men.
   c) Intellectual Dishonesty – the failure to conform his own thinking to certain immutable facts of existence. The holding of contradictions.

6) The practice of these problems are called the Primary Vices. The practice of Primary Vices leads to the practice of numerous Derivative Vices, both of thought and action.

7) The counter to vice is the practice of certain mental states called the Primary Virtues. The practice of the Primary Virtues leads to numerous Derivative Virtues, both of thought and action. The Primary Virtues are:
   a) Intellectual Independence
   b) Intellectual Curiosity
   c) Intellectual Honesty

8) The successful practice of virtue, along with his understanding of the fundamental nature of existence (metaphysics) and his knowledge of how he thinks and knows things (epistemology), gives a man what is called Rationality

9) With his rationality a man then develops his Powers, which he will need to successfully support his own life and deal satisfactorily with other men.

PART 4: POLITICS
(The Normal Psychology Of The Individual <u>IN</u> Relation To Others)

**FIRST THEY CAME FOR THE SOCIALISTS, AND I DID NOT SPEAK OUT,
FOR I WAS NOT A SOCIALIST.
THEN THEY CAME FOR THE TRADE UNIONISTS, AND I DID NOT SPEAK OUT,
FOR I WAS NOT A TRADE UNIONIST.
THEN THEY CAME FOR THE JEWS, AND I DID NOT SPEAK OUT,
FOR I WAS NOT A JEW.
THEN THEY CAME FOR ME,
AND THERE WAS NO ONE LEFT TO SPEAK FOR ME.**
Martin Niemoller

**THERE'S A NEW JERRY FALWELL DOLL OUT.
YOU WIND IT UP AND IT STICKS IT'S
NOSE IN EVERYBODY'S BUSINESS.**
Johnny Carson

In the previous Part on Ethics, we discussed how man is faced with the fundamental choice of either living as Intellectually Independent or, (ultimately), as a Collectivist. We showed how it is right for an individual man to live **Rationally** as Intellectually Independent, Curious, and Honest. The question in Politics now becomes: Is what is best for an individual man **in conflict** with what is best for man in his relation to others? The answer is – **no, it is not in conflict!**

In a manner similar to Ethics, in his relations with others man is faced with two fundamental choices, as follows: **1)** he may (attempt to) cooperate as collectivists, or **2)** he may cooperate as individualists. If the reader thinks that cooperation as collectivists would be best for man, he would be wrong for the following simple reason. In a collectivist society the more clever, powerful, selfish, and corrupted individuals will always FOOL the less clever individuals, thereby taking advantage of them, and ultimately enslaving them. The remainder of this Part, and much of that one following, is devoted to explaining the ins and outs all this.

Before discussing politics proper it is important to remind ourselves that, aside from any interactions with one another, each man is already dealing with

63

his own ethical (i.e. personal) issues **which he brings to his dealings with others.** As there is a wide range of success among men at dealing with their own personal challenges, so there is a wide range of skills and abilities that men carry to their dealings with others. Dealing with others can be both a great benefit for a man or a great danger – therefore, a proper politics will provide for both the **free interactions between men AND their protection from treachery and the errors of other men, to the extent practical.**

To tell the truth, there is a **conspiracy of sorts,** never spoken, which goes something like this – "I am more fearful of your freedom than of my enslavement. Therefore, we will use social pressure, and social force (government), to destroy our freedom; then I will just take back the freedoms that I like." -- the result being that all social conflicts are nothing but the struggle over **who is to be free and who is to be enslaved.** A vicious circle exists where each man expects (correctly) that if he allows other men their freedom the favor will not be returned.

In the conventional point of view "politics" is a view of the needs, or wants, of "society" to which the individual shall conform. Such a viewpoint is obviously collectivist and requires the sacrifice of the individual to the alleged interests of some group – which ever group happens to be in power; so such a point of view is highly suspect. I have demonstrated that it is the individual that exercises volition, that a man's conclusions are his guides to action, and that a man must survive by his own effort. Therefore, in reality, it is the other way around -- a proper politics is a view of the needs of the individual to which society should conform. The topic of Politics is properly understood as **the study of the rules which shall govern all human interactions.**

Consider the following sampling of questions:
1) What is a "right"? What is "freedom"?
2) What do you have a right to expect of others?
3) What do others have a right to expect of you?
4) Are there things that all men should be able to agree on?
5) What should be the rules for social agreement and interaction?
6) Is man a "social animal"? In what way?
7) To what degree has the U.S. departed from its Constitution?
8) How can one properly evaluate politicians?
9) (you fill in her)

To all these questions, and many more, will be provided answers.

YOU CAN'T CHEAT AN HONEST MAN.
                                        Unknown

THE PROBLEM ISN'T THAT YOU'RE PLAYING A GAME YOU CAN'T WIN,
IT'S THAT YOU'RE PLAYING A GAME THEY CAN'T LOSE.
                                        The Author

Though in the end Albert Einstein's ideas on government per se (i.e., social force) fell short, a man's intellectual shortcomings do not negate his real intellectual successes, (including, hopefully, those of this author). The following excerpt from a 1934, Einstein essay, was for the most part a success:

> "When we survey our lives and endeavors, we soon observe that almost the whole of our actions and desires is bound up with the existence of other human beings. We notice that our whole nature resembles that of the social animals. We eat food that others have produced, wear clothes that others have made, live in houses that others have built. The greater part of our knowledge and beliefs has been communicated to us by other people through the medium of language which others have created. Without language our mental capacities would be poor indeed, comparable to those of the higher animals; we have, therefore, to admit that we owe our principle advantage over the beasts to the fact of living in human society. The individual, if left alone from birth, would remain primitive and beastlike in his thoughts and feelings to a degree that we can hardly conceive. The individual is what he is and has the significance that he is not so much in virtue of his individuality, but rather as a member of the great human community, which directs his material and spiritual existence from the cradle to the grave.

> "A man's value to the community depends primarily on how far his feelings, thoughts, and actions are directed toward promoting the good of his fellows. We call him good or bad according to his attitude in this respect. It looks **at first sight** (emphasis mine) as if our estimate of a man depended entirely on his social qualities. And yet such an attitude would be wrong. It can be easily seen that all the valuable achievements, material, spiritual and moral, which we receive from society have been brought about in the course of countless generations by creative individuals. Someone once discovered the use of fire, someone the cultivation of edible plants, and someone the

steam engine. Only the individual can think, and thereby create new values for society, nay, even set up new moral standards to which the life of the community conforms. Without creative personalities able to think and judge independently, the upward development of society is as unthinkable as the development of the individual personality without the nourishing soil of the community.

"The health of society thus depends quite as much on the independence of the individuals composing it as on their close social cohesion. It has been rightly said that the very basis of the Greco-European-American culture, and in particular of its brilliant flowering in the Italian Renaissance, which put an end to the stagnation of medieval Europe, has been the liberation and comparative isolation of the individual."

Albert Einstein
Essay: "Society and Personality", 1934

Note: The above is the full quote by Einstein. I have seen the second and third paragraphs omitted by collectivists, obviously to promote their agenda.

And so we ask – what should be the rules for social interaction which would promote both "close social cohesion" **and** the freedom and development of the individual? To arrive at the correct answers to this problem we must ask the right questions and consider the right facts.

In the Part 3, we studied Ethics because man has no automatic knowledge of dealing with problems faced by himself as an individual. To properly conceptualize Ethics we began at the beginning by considering man's problems in the widest possible sense. In this Part we study Politics because man has no automatic understanding of dealing properly with others. Specifically, man has no **social instinct,** yet there are still **things and behaviors that he wants and needs from others.** We begin at the beginning and this is the crucial starting point of Politics. If there were no "things and behaviors that men wanted and needed from one another" there would be no social interaction and no need for a politics; men would be mostly indifferent towards one another and that would be the end of it. So, in Politics we begin by considering "the things and behaviors that men want and need from one another" in the **widest possible sense,** from the unfamiliar fellow citizen one meets on the street to one's most intimate relationships.

So, before moving on, really get this – **anyone** who has more than the most passing interest in you wants some thing, or behavior from you. This is not wrong. It is the way it is. The questions to be asked are not whether a man wants something; but rather, **what** does he want from others?, **how** does he intend on getting it?, and whether a mutually desirable interaction can be worked out. It is to these questions that the study of Politics is addressed.

So, how do individuals interact to acquire the "things and behaviors that they want and need from one another"? We use the observation and integration skills we identified in Part 2, and count three ways.

3. PHYSICAL FORCE -   This is the widely understood method of getting one person to comply with another's wishes.

2. MATERIAL TRADE -   We shall call this the **economic** power.
This is the power one has by virtue of having things, or potential behaviors, that others want or need. It is the method of **trading** things and behaviors with others for things and behaviors that we want and need from them. This power is much more than mere money. It includes EVERYTHING that is not physical force or intellectual power. Please understand this and keep it in mind. Economics is the "meat and potatoes" of man's life with others and is a very large topic.

1. THE INTELLECT – This is the power of persuasion that men can possess to influence others.   Examples include: Leadership, Charisma, Teacher-Student relationships, Parent-Child relationships, Counselor-Client, writers, speakers, all of one's experience, knowledge and wisdom, etc.

We define that which men use in order to acquire the "things and behaviors that they want and need" as **Power.**

So we have the potential powers that man possess, listed and defined:

1. Intellectual Power (Persuasion)
2. Economic Power   (Material Trade)
3. Physical Force

The powers are listed in a definite order. In the listing order, number Three does not mean "bad" but "easy", and number One does not mean "good" but "hard". All three powers are "good" and can be misused. All three powers are **active** in man's life at all times, however, in any particular relationship one of the powers is **dominant** while the other two lie in the **background.** For example, if I buy something from you in your store the dominant power is economic, however, that relationship is backed up by the Founding of our country, granting the people free trade, which was intellectual in nature (Power 1), and also by the police who will come and get me if I leave your store without paying you (Power 3).

The higher one moves up the power structure the more difficult is the power to practice well. Many people practice as little integrity as they can get away with in life. Therefore, the following is another crucial point -- when the people in a particular relationship endeavor to allow two or more powers to be dominant in that relationship, the **lower power tends to "eat" the higher power,** thereby destroying the blessings of the higher power. Any person who insists on having more than one power be dominant in a relationship probably intends on having the lowest one dominate once the other person is "committed to" (i.e. trapped in) the relationship. Naturally it follows that if any of the powers are lacking in a man, or if the man refuses to adequately exercise them, then the use of another power is to be expected. For example, if a man has nothing to offer for trade in a relationship, (or refuses to be a trader), he must then resort to either intellectual persuasion or some form of force. More often than not he will lead with the promise of some form of intellectual persuasion, and then when one is not looking, or else in a weakened position, he will betray. Another widespread example are people who are deficient intellectually yet attempt to rear children – they deal with the children primarily on the levels of materialism and force – the child's needs for intellectual example remain unmet.

In Part 3 (Ethics) it was proposed that all problems faced by the individual, **as an individual,** are traceable to, **1)** the failure to adequately distance one's mind from the minds of others, **2)** the failure to deal adequately with nature itself (including the people in it and their behaviors), and **3)** the failure to deal honestly with one's own ideas. Likewise, in Politics it is proposed that all struggles between men are **due to unwise, misuse, or abuse of power.**

Observe the following chart as a teaching aid:

1. Intellectual Powers

Allows/Promotes man's free will

2. Economic Power

----

3. Physical Force   Negates man's free will

     Previously, it was suggested that man's volition **is** his power of reason as a man. Therefore, we seek the rules for human interactions which control Force in a society, while promoting Trade and Rationality. Rationality is quite literally the **opposite** of Force. The more Force there is for an individual, or society, the less Rationality there will be (other things being equal), and vice versa.

     Using the observation and integration techniques theorized in Part 2, we make the following observations regarding power:

1.   Once an entity is granted a certain power we must expect that entity to exercise the power **fully.** In human relationships it is often an appropriate, compassionate, or loving thing to not fully exercise a power, but we must be prepared for the full exercise of the power.

2.   Once an entity is granted a certain power the entity has the **right** to exercise the power.

3.   Intellectual Power implies full freedom of the intellect – the freedom of thought, gathering information and knowledge, and expressing that knowledge in any form. There must be no forced censorship of any kind. Else would be a contradiction.

4.   The Economic Power implies full property rights. If an entity has the power to exercise trade, then the entity must have something to trade. If the entity may exercise the power fully, then the entity must have full use of property. Else would be a contradiction.

5.   Power cannot be "shared". Such would be a contradiction. If an entity has the right to exercise a power fully, then there can be no shared power.

6.	Since power cannot be shared, property cannot be shared or "communally owned". If property is jointly produced, each producer owns his "share" of the property. One does not get to communally own property – such would represent a complete loss for the producer of the property and a complete gain for the non- producer, rendering the producer with no property and nothing to trade. **A man without property is a beggar.**

7.	The entity which produced property can never be changed. Property may be given, or traded, or taken or stolen, but this does not change who produced the property.

8.	Property must remain under the sole control of the producer of the property until it is given or traded.

9.	For various reasons, power is not evenly distributed among men. Therefore, this is a crucial reason why physical force must be banned from human interactions while individuals shall have the right to exercise the other powers fully and with no interference.

In considering all of the foregoing, we see at once the precarious situation of man as an intelligent being -- the roots of the "endless cycles of hope and despair". The task for social man is of power management in human affairs. How is man to manage power among men?

RIGHTS

We seek to promote rationality and trade, while controlling the **arbitrary use of force** in the lives of men. This is accomplished through the concept of **rights.** Since there are three fundamental powers, there are three rights:

POWER	RIGHT
Intellectual	Complete freedom of thought and expression. No censorship
Economic	Complete freedom of production, ownership and trade
Force	Freedom from all force. All human actions voluntary

The above are the ideas we seek to enact. There has never been a significant society that has provided such full freedom to all its people, and at this point it is only a concept. This Book was written in the hope of helping and enlightening those who read it. Beyond that, we can only make the attempt at improving our lives together, but the lack of a fully free society will be a constant source of interference and frustration.

The three rights, or freedoms, are discussed briefly.

1.   Freedom from force:

This we shall call "fundamental freedom", or "political freedom". He who uses physical force against any other person thereby denies that person his freedoms and rights. Further, physical force is the only way to deny an **adult** his rights. Absent physical force a man is left free to choose and live his life as he sees fit. Therefore, the banning of physical force in private relations among adults is necessary AND SUFFICIENT for securing all of man's rights. This is done by forming a government to enforce that concept within a given geographical area. The government is formed and ceded the power only to punish those who use physical force against others. The government never initiates force itself. Under such a government all actions that do not use physical force against others are LEGAL. The government never injects itself into the affairs of the people other than to perform its basic function. It does not gather or store any information on the people not needed to directly perform its duties. It does not surveil the citizens without warrant. It minds its business! In particular, such a proper government does not participate in any way in the economic or intellectual affairs of the people, i.e., "power cannot be shared". It may coin money but it does not manipulate its value. It may enforce free trade but not restrict such among its people. It operates no centers of learning and has nothing to say about education. It does not fight "wars" on disease, drugs, poverty, ignorance or invisible enemies. "A proper government is based on a definite ideology, but must play no role in promoting that ideology." (Frank Meyer, In Defense Of Freedom, 1962).

The determination of what a proper government should do, and how to finance it, is a very complex subject belonging to the field of political science, and **certainly not as that field is practiced today.** At the extreme minimalist end of the spectrum there is some room for honest discussion and disagreement, but nothing like the bickering, polarization and massive governments we see in the world today.

A widespread notion has been that there ought be a "separation of powers" **within government,** which supposedly protects its citizens. This was a tragic misconception. Although a proper government does perform three logical functions, it being important to keep them separate, in fact the whole of a proper government exercises only one power – the power of using force to prohibit the **arbitrary** use of force among its citizens. And since power cannot be shared, the REAL separation of powers, the one that mattered, was the separation of powers **between** the people and their government – with the government exercising its specific power and the people exercising all other powers. Kings, dictators, and politicians under-stand that power cannot be shared and take care to enforce law and order upon the citizens, though not so much upon themselves. They understand that the citizens cannot be allowed to steal each other's property, for then what would be left for the government to steal? The recent late-2020 riots in the U.S., **permitted by state and local governments**, are not a disproof of this, but an **example of it!** As soon as the Left consolidates its power "law and order" will be ruthlessly restored upon the regular citizens, and only expression of its power will be permitted. (As I write, the government is planning a new FBI building twice the size of the Pentagon.) The State is currently in the final stages of usurping the Economic and Intellectual Powers, (if one hadn't noticed). It is never one another that the citizens of a society need fear the most, but rather **groups of others acting through their own government.** It is just this division of power between the people and the government and which the Founders of the United States were attempting to establish with the Constitution.

Another widespread misconception has been that a **free society** can be established by military means and maintained primarily by the police

72

power. This is not true and has never been the case. It is true that military action may be used to destroy some existing order, or drive out intruders, but only the intellectual power could establish a **new free order.** Likewise, in maintaining a free society, the police power not backed up by adequate intellect by the people will fail.

2. **Freedom of production, ownership and trade:**
The freedom from force fully accounts and provides for freedom of production, ownership and trade. If a man is free from force he is necessarily free to work and create property, keep that property and dispose of it as he sees fit. Free from force, he also necessarily controls his own body and life and may live as he sees fit. Nevertheless, it is useful to identify this freedom and discuss it for clarity since so many men think, or act, as if controlling a man's production, ownership, and trade is not force.

3. **Freedom of the intellect:**
Likewise, there are men who believe that controlling, with force, the intellectual materials that a man produces or consumes, is not force. Therefore, it is useful to separately identify this freedom as well. Further, children are born into this world helpless, not only materially, but intellectually too. Being fully free means being free to develop and exercise all of one's economic and intellectual powers. Caretakers who do not provide their proteges with the necessary **material** needs can, rightfully, run afoul the law. But because of the fact of human volition, it would be impractical or inappropriate to legislate the intellectual activities of men – even such relations between caretakers and proteges. A child's intellect can be destroyed by the irrationality of those around him – and it is **perfectly legal to do so.** There are men -- many, many men -- whose ability to reason is so damaged that their recovery or improvement is never to be expected, certainly not amid their social existence with all of their irrational peers. So the intellects of children are an area of special concern regarding freedom of the intellect.

These things, and much more, are characteristic of a free society under a proper government. It is not within the scope of this Book to exhaustively discuss the features of a proper government, nor to discuss certain areas of honest disagreement among rational men regarding a number of very difficult issues. My purpose is to present a vision which provides the reader with a more rational starting point for thinking and discussion. As previously pointed out, it is preferable to debate with another who **does accept logical conclusions**, yet has reservations about applying them, than it is to argue with another who does not deal in logical conclusions to begin with. In fact, when one detects that another is not attempting to deal in logical conclusions, serious conversation is over!

THE MOST FUNDAMENTAL PROBLEM IN POLITICS IS NOT THE CONTROL
OF WICKEDNESS, BUT THE LIMITATION OF RIGHTEOUSNESS.
Henry Kissinger
From: The Coming Anarchy
Robert D. Kaplan

FREEDOM ULTIMATELY MEANS THE RIGHT OF OTHER PEOPLE
TO DO THINGS YOU DON'T APPROVE OF.
Thomas Sowell

VIRTUE, POWER AND HAPPINESS

The goal of a man's life is properly his true happiness. We now simply point out that the path, the only path, to happiness begins with the practice of virtue – the Virtues we have been discussing and explaining at length in this Book. The practice of the Virtues leads then (other things being equal) to a man's powers – intellectual and economic – also which we have been explaining at length. The man then applies his powers to achieve his goals and, (again, other things being equal), chooses to be happy.

POWER - METAPHYSICALLY GIVEN and ACQUIRED EXPENDABLE and NON-EXPENDABLE

Because man exists in both physical and intellectual states he has powers which were both given to him as a "gift" of his nature, as well as those developed by himself through his intellect. Because of men's individual natures, as well as their own efforts, power will not be evenly distributed among men. Nevertheless, a man's powers are his and his alone, and they must not be taken from him nor should he be prohibited their full use if the man so chooses. In this state the man is said to be **free.**

74

A further distinction between powers could be made that they come in two kinds – expendable and non-expendable. Expendable powers are those which, upon use, leave less of the power than existed before. Expendable powers tend to be the **material things** a man possesses, but not always. Conversely, non-expendable powers are those that a man may exercise relatively freely with no depletion of the power. Non-expendable powers tend to be the **behaviors** in which a man can engage, but not always. This distinction regarding powers is of particular interest for close personal relationships. It would seem that the best close relationships would be those which **emphasize** the non-expendable powers, with them being freely shared.

NON-CONCEPTUAL MENTALITY IN-COMPATIBLE WITH FREEDOM

IT IS EASIER TO FOOL A MAN THAN CONVINCE HIM
THAT HE HAS BEEN FOOLED.
Mark Twain

I AM FREE AND THAT IS WHY I AM LOST.
Franz Kafka

In this modern world a man is faced with a myriad of choices simply regarding his **material** existence – what things, or situations, does he want and should he strive for? Though even in this the irrational man of today experiences a bewilderment or anxiety, the situation is even worse to the extent of his **political freedom;** for the politically free man experiences also choices concerning his **being!** – his choices concerning the exercise (or not) of the Primary Virtues, the development of Derivative Virtues (or not), and in the details of his dealings with other men. To the extent that a man is not free these decisions might be made for him. Should the man take up drinking or smoking or other drugs? Should he acquire higher education, or not? Should he save more money now, or spend more? Should he pursue a singular career, or enjoy a variety of jobs? Should he work towards a retirement, or just "wing it"? Should he follow the crowd, or make his own way? What knowledge should he pursue, and how much? How many, and how deep, does he want his relationships to be? How rational should the man aspire to be?

The **irrational** (and free) man experiences an anxiety is his freedom of choices. To alleviate this anxiety regarding **material choices,** most irrational men respond by **wanting more** – more things and situations than needed for their survival and happiness (if provided by others, so much the better); although a few men will develop an **irrational desire for little,** i.e., to "live off the grid".

However, with regard to anxiety **concerning their being,** most irrational men respond by desiring less -- **less freedom!** Without realizing it or thinking the matter through, men take steps to lessen their freedom. At the personal level men will take steps to give up their power of choice. At the level of society, men will desire, nay demand!, the **destruction of the choices of others!** ("The irrational man is more fearful of other's freedom than of his own enslavement.") A moments reflection will reveal that the consequences for a society of men's wanting **more things and less freedom** are like attempting to put out a fire with gasoline!

A quote on this matter is so relevant that it is well worth repeating here:

> "Almost a decade back, in New Delhi, I went to a speech on "freedom" by Andrew Cohen, an American Spiritual teacher. The speech was about how our worldviews imprison us. He challenged us to recognize that despite the way we talk about freedom, somewhere in our minds we do not want to be free. That we so closely identify ourselves with our material possessions, social prestige and our pathological need for external validation that we make ourselves puppets of other people's agendas. That by covering our insecurities in drama, we manipulate others to serve our ulterior purposes, and eventually wind our minds into knots. That as a result, we have a complicated society where everyone wants to be free, but everyone also wants to control others."
>
> Liberty Magazine
> July 2006
> Jayant Bhandari
> "The Books Of Summer"

In fact, this desire for only limited freedom is so widespread among men that we observe the following world-wide phenomenon: In countries with more oppressive governments we see that the people tend to be more **socially permissive** (including sexually), while in countries with more "political freedom" we see greater tendency toward **social control of behavior** (particularly sexual activity). Something like this did not escape the attention of George Orwell in Nineteen Eighty-Four – he writes of the totalitarian regime, in part:

76

"In all questions of morals (the commoners) were allowed to follow their ancestral code. The sexual puritanism of the Party was not imposed upon them. Promiscuity went unpunished; divorce was permitted. For that matter, even religious worship would have been permitted if (the commoners) had shown any sign of needing or wanting it. They were **beneath** suspicion. As the Party slogan put it: "(Commoners) and animals are free." (emphasis mine)

Nor did the observation escape Einstein:

"Here (in Princeton), the people who compose what is called 'society' enjoy even less freedom than their counterparts in Europe. Yet they seem unaware of this restriction since their way of life tends to inhibit personality development from childhood."

Einstein: The Life And Times
Ronald W. Clark

We once met an Argentinian who was travelling around the world on his motorcycle, and asked him how many women he had had? He said that he had stopped counting.

The root of anxiety regarding life choices goes back to the lack of a proper concept structure in man. The rational man's concepts simplify a seemingly complicated life and render it **livable!** But for the non-conceptual man life is not so livable. And, finally, it is said that "power corrupts", or that "money is the root of all evil". Such notions are actually false, and appear true only to the extent that a man who is **already irrational,** (i.e., practicing the primary vices), acquires power.

TIME VALUE RELATIONSHIPS

Thus far, this Book has been devoted to helping men improve their relationships with one another and achieve more satisfaction from them – but not from the **time value aspect**. Although many human relationships naturally happen over time, this issue still needs special attention. The present topic is for filling that gap. As always, we begin by respecting the distinction between the metaphysically given and the man-made --there are things that man cannot change and things that he can.

Life would be lonely indeed, and little would be accomplished, if all human interactions were chance encounters. In his **own unique way**, man is certainly a social animal. There are great benefits of having relationships with others that happen over time. We don't change our place of work each day, we don't search for new friends or loved ones every day, discarding the old ones, and our children are pretty much our children for keeps. So man needs satisfactory time value relationships, and the inability to maintain them is a major source of trouble for him. On the other hand, as a man develops relationships with certain others he must by necessity forgo relationships with "other" others since he does not live forever – a man must make choices even in this, since his time on Earth is limited.

It was previously emphasized that the whole purpose of a Politics is to promote the benefits of human relationships while simultaneously protecting a man from the errors or treachery of other men. Both of these purposes must be given their due weight by a Politics **or it is not a Politics, but a con game.** A Politics must respect **the individual man** – his virtues, his powers, his property, his rights, his life. Once the element of time is added to a relationship the potential for errors, abuse and loss increase exponentially! Further, since there is nothing to add to the benefits of human interactions other than the free exercise of men's virtues and powers (which have already been covered), the only remaining issues to be discussed in this Topic are that of **risk** and **protection.**

It is important to pause and re-emphasize another point made earlier. The **vision for man** described in this Book has never existed in any society – ever – but only in the minds of a relatively few thinkers, and perhaps a few nuclear families. There are no "good old days" which I am attempting to return to when my group had an **unjust** advantage -- for that would be a con, and this Book is not a con. I also stated in the beginning that this Book would be "solution oriented" rather than "problem oriented". Therefore I won't go back and rehash all of the traditions, errors, evils and persecutions of men in the past, nor would that even be possible. In this Book **I am simply pointing out what would work now.**

The first issue to set aside is: what must a man expect to risk in his time value relationships? The ideal to which we shall aspire will be that a man shall be expected to risk only those things that are metaphysically unavoidable. Nature makes sense and is perfect, and man does right by conforming to it. Man is not victimized by nature but by other men! If man can create man-made institutions which provide for reduced risk in his time value relationships then this might be good and appropriate. But time value relationships are not a primary but a derivative of man's intelligence -- he does not have the right to create institutions which **increase** risk of loss for **individual men.**

So what are the various risks that man should expect in his time value relationships? Obviously, the most precious and irreplaceable thing he risks **is time itself.** If men lived forever then time loss would not be an issue. It is a metaphysically given fact that men can change their minds, pursue dead-end leads, fail in their various endeavors, etc., since men are not infallible. So it would be irrational to expect to not risk a part of one's life in the pursuit of any relationship. Likewise, it follows that when dealing with a **rational** other person it should be taken as a supreme compliment, and sign of hope and courage, if another is willing to risk **their precious time** on a relationship with oneself. While, by the same token, one should be cautious of attempts by another to reduce their own risk of time without a corresponding reduction of one's own risk. Obviously, as a man gets older, his time more precious, and the wasting of his time more hurtful.

The second unavoidable risk for men in their time value relationships is **disappointment.** Since a relationship can be very important to a man, yet fail, a man can be greatly disappointed. This is an unavoidable fact of life that a man must simply accept. Perhaps the cause of the failed involvement is rational, perhaps not, nevertheless it hurts all the same.

Since men are fallible, irrational, dishonest, a man also risks **material loss** in his dealings with others. It is to this we now turn.

Men may have **implicit** time value relationships with one another. Such relationships are based on things such as mutual understanding, admiration, trust, respect, shared interests and endeavors. Depending on the presence of these qualities the time value nature of the relationship may be very powerful, reliable -- yet it remains informal. In such a relationship a man will likely expend some material values, and may even explicitly risk them as a token of good will and trust. However, since the relationship is informal, the rule for material values remains -- possession is, or should be, 100% of the law. In the informal relationship there is no legal recourse for redress in a civil court. In a dispute between men in such a relationship they simply part ways if a mutually agreeable solution is not found. However, as the value of risked materials becomes greater, and/or the **level of trust decreases,** men may choose to formalize their endeavor.

CONTRACTUAL TIME VALUE RELATIONSHIPS

One valid institution which man may create is a system of law which respects and enforces private contracts between men. Men may **choose** to enter private contracts with other men. The contract is for the protection of men's material interests in the context of their time value relationships. These private contracts are an expression of the **economic power** – and recall that power cannot be shared. The economic power is properly held by the people, not the government. It is the people who approach the government with a private contract – **the government does not approach the people with a law!**

There are three types of contractual agreements, all dealing men's material interests. This is the origin of that old saying "you can't mix love and money". (In truth you CAN mix love and money, just not by contract!). The three types of contracts are:

Contracts for repayment: This is when **existing** material property is "loaned" by one man to another. The borrower promises to repay the borrowed value at some point in the future.

Contracts for production: This is an agreement between men to jointly produce **new** property. The contract specifies the expectations of each party to it and what portion of the values thus produced will become the property of each man.

Contracts specifying behaviors: This is an agreement between men **agreeing to certain behaviors.** This contract may be enacted alone or in combination with agreements for repayment and/or production. To clarify this type of contract only by way of one example: When a group of **prospective employees** having this type of contract approach some **employer,** stating that they will only deal with him on terms acceptable to the group as a whole, their contract has been called a "collective bargaining agreement". At such a point the employer **does not yet have a contract for production** with the group, nor should he be forced to make one. The collective bargaining agreement merely states, among the employees, that they will either all work for him, or none of them will.

Contracts may specify measures to be taken in the event of a dispute or default. The government simply enforces the contract impartially and generally has no say in what men may agree to in their contracts. Eventualities not covered in the contract are settled impartially at the discretion of a judge or jury.

One final point of clarification must be mentioned prior to moving on. A man only risks losing material things that are **already his property.** The prospect of **not gaining** material values that yet belong to another is not a "risk", although this attitude is widespread in society.

INDENTURED SERVITUDE

I AM, SOMEHOW, LESS INTERESTED IN THE WEIGHT AND CONVOLUTIONS OF EINSTEIN'S BRAIN THAN THE NEAR CERTAINTY THAT PEOPLE OF EQUAL TALENT HAVE LIVED AND DIED IN COTTON FIELDS AND SWEATSHOPS.
Stephen J. Gould

The reader might think it unnecessary to further elaborate on the topic of slavery since the point of this entire Part has been on how to banish it. However, to be completely clear I must discuss the concept of **indentured servitude.** If the reader thinks this institution to be only of another time, or place, he is mistaken. Though the overt forms of this practice have been eliminated from "civilized" societies, it still exists, though in a more hidden form.

To see that indentured servitude, as a form of slavery, still exists, let us **conceptualize it.** I offer two real-life examples from history; **A)** a young man wishes to practice some trade, yet he is prohibited, **by some law or other social force,** from just learning the trade somehow by his own wits (working in the trade, reading books, acquiring equipment, etc.) and going into business. Instead the man is required to "apprentice" himself (a government made law or contract) to an existing tradesman for a legally defined period of time. Or suppose, **B)** a man lives in an oppressive and unfree country to the extent that he cannot accumulate any property in a meaningful sense – the man's life is a waste. But he sees, across the Atlantic Ocean, a country where he might live for himself. His only way to pay his way there is to "indenture" himself to someone who can pay his way.

In both the above examples, and numerous possible others, two common factors define the indentured servitude: **1)** The man was denied, by some force, the full use of his rights and economic and/or intellectual powers, then **2)** The man was thereby coerced into some enforceable contract or agreement, quite disadvantageous to him, that he likely would not have entered had he not been denied the full use of his rights or powers in the first place. In the first example

81

both the force and the indentured servitude occurred in country "A"; while in the second example the force was committed in country "A", while the indentured servitude occurred in country "B". In both cases, however, the evil lied not in the contract of servitude per se, but in the **denial of a man the full use of his freedom and powers**.

Close examination will show that, in every case, the particular rights forcefully denied of men will be just those needed to coerce the individual into the, so called, "contracts". The greatest injustice is committed not against the many, many weak men who submit to the pressure into servitude, but against the **few great men who resist.** A man's "society" does not get to determine which of his rights, needs or powers are dispensable – **only the man!** As long as men are not fully free there is indentured servitude as a form of slavery. When a single person coerces another into servitude it's called a "crime", but when a group does it, it's called "legislation".

Having discussed Ethics and Politics each at some length, we are now in position to cover several additional important points before closing this Part on man in his relation to others.

A FEW WORDS REGARDING NEEDS AND WANTS

Strictly speaking, the private determination by a man as to what are his wants and what are his needs is an **ethical** (private) question and not a **political** (interpersonal) one. A man is no more entitled from others to his needs as he is to his wants. Few people would argue that men do not have both "needs" and "wants", and that certain things or conditions clearly fall into one court or the other. Obviously, a man needs the proverbial "food, clothing and shelter", however, to limit man's needs to these would be treating him as an animal.

Man is different from other animals. Although the rational man "lives in the moment" as they say, he is keenly aware of his future as well, and practices what has been termed, (pejoratively by some), a "future time orientation". Further, man's emotions are fundamentally for the purpose of promoting his physical survival and happiness, and **are interpreted as such.** Since man must emote in order to accomplish anything at all, it follows that to define man's needs as only food, clothing and shelter is to condemn him to only emoting regarding those things, and then only PURSUING those things, and thus relegating him to an animals existence. The preceding chain of reasoning shows that we must

82

allow man to **experience** as "needs" things other than only that needed for his physical survival. When a rational man wants something he **wants** it. What man does have some control over are **the things that he wants.** By similar reasoning, it would be wrong to expect a man to change his wants "nilly willy", based simply on what is available, (or merely on what is offered him) – this would not be "wanting" in the human sense at all.

The way that a rational man determines what are his needs and wants is not arbitrary, but neither are the conclusions identical among men. A rational man surveys his fixed needs, interests, skills and abilities and sets a hierarchy of goals somewhere beyond his mere survival. The man needs to feel competent. The man needs to achieve his goals. This does not mean that the man will achieve his goals or that he has the "right" to achieve them, but only that he has the right to try and, if he succeeds, to enjoy their achievement.

LOVE

People, people who need people,
Are the luckiest people in the world.
                Bob Merrill, Jule Styne
                "Funny Girl"

Without You
Life Has No Meaning Or Rhyme,
Like Notes To A Song Out Of Time.
How Can I Repay
You For Having Faith
In Me?
                Thom Bell, Linda Creed
                The Stylistics

We will now address the topic of **Love** within the present context. People ask what is love, and how might it be maintained? Some people seem to have love, yet are unable to explain to others how they created it. Can we apply our rational approach and give the reader some useful knowledge on even this topic? I think so.

The first point to settle is to define love. I attempted to compile an elaborate argument to prove that love is an emotion, but aborted the effort as it was not working, and instead elected to pursue a simple definitional approach. I have been around for a while and the only alternative definition I have encountered was that love is a person's ACTIONS toward another. It is true that in a love relationship many good things and behaviors are exchanged, however, this seems to be circular reasoning since our definition of ALL rational human interaction

83

consists of just that – the exchange of material and/or intellectual values, (Oh shucks, did I just prove that love is an emotion?).

So we will proceed on the presumption that love is an emotion -- a strong emotion -- a strong LASTING emotion.

Running the emotion through our "emotion analyzer", we see that the emotion is regarding something that is "good for you", it is "outside of you", and it is a reward for successful action. Further, recall that the fundamental cause of all human interactions is the things and behaviors that men seek from one another. Therefore, **love is the emotion one has toward another person who provides something that one values.** Using the observational and integration techniques theorized in Part 2, we arrive at the following requirements causing the emotion of love, as opposed to mere "like", or "friendship", or perhaps a satisfying business relationship:

1. **What one seeks from the other must be a rational "need"**, else how could the feeling thus caused be reliably strong and lasting? The rational man has needs beyond the proverbial "food, clothing and shelter", but are not determined on whim either. The rational man surveys his life and carefully selects the things he will value in all of his pursuits, but particularly those he seeks from others.

2. **The things or behaviors sought must be things that only another person can provide** and not something that one can provide for oneself. Again, else how could the feeling thus produced be strong and lasting. Interestingly, all things being equal, in a free society, providing one's own food, clothing and shelter is easy (for the rational man), so this pretty much rules out these needs for causing love. Therefore, a real love relationship is built on higher things than mere needs for survival of the body.

3. **Whatever one values and seeks from the other, one must never become entitled to it.** Once one becomes entitled to the things or behaviors that are sought, then it is no longer the other person providing them, but oneself. Another person giving one things not by choice is not giving them, but rather being taken from. **The feeling thus produced will not be love but hate.**

It is important to re-emphasize a point about emotions, including love. For the rational man emotions are motivators and rewards. The rational man is mindful that, though in a superficial sense he "acts in pursuit of pleasant

84

emotions", on a deeper level he is really pursuing the things he values and gets love, love of the other person, as a reward for a rational life. Love is the emotion of **gratitude** when directed towards another person, or persons.

Because the feeling of love (properly understood) is but a form of gratitude, and not merely a self-indulgence, it is honorable to wish to preserve it. How is the feeling of love maintained? One gets up each morning and considers those he loves, how they provide things and behaviors that he needs, which he cannot provide for himself, and to which he is not entitled. Here is another way to look at love – it is the PRICE one pays for allowing oneself to be dependent upon another person for a need to which one never becomes entitled. And it is a price that a man had better pay! Can one love more than one person? Most certainly.

> COMPATIBILITY IS AS MUCH AN ACHIEVEMENT IN A
> RELATIONSHIP AS A PRECONDITION FOR IT.
> The Author

The lover wishes to maintain the feeling of love, but the lover also needs to experience **being loved.** Therefore, love **must be expressed, and in a way which is meaningful to the beloved.** In fact, when all other materialistic B.S. is removed, it is these expressions that are the real reasons why men love one another. In 1992, Gary Chapman published The Five Love Languages. It is likely that this book is responsible for saving many loves and relationships. In his book Chapman identifies the five most common or important expressions of love that people need to **receive** in a close love relationship. But the bottom line is that a man who wishes to feel love has a **moral duty to himself and the beloved** to express it also -- and with gladness in his heart!

One final word about making love last. It is a good thing for relationships and love to continue. Good people, particularly in this day and age, can be hard to find. Going through life with a constant carousel of different people is no way to live. A man needs to be close to a few people. But relationships do not always last. There are any number of reasons why men part ways – some rational, some not. Eventually, even in a perfect relationship, someone will die. Not the longevity of an involvement, nor the particular things exchanged, have any bearing whatsoever on creation of the emotion of love. As long as the three criteria of my suggestions are met in the relationship it is REAL love, and the love will continue after the involvement is gone – after all, it really is the other person that one loves.

THE ESTHETIC ASPECT OF RELATIONSHIPS

Previously it was described how when the rational man looks out upon nature, and sees that he is conforming to it, the emotion of "satisfaction" is produced. This was called the "esthetic response". It was pointed out how, all things being equal, the more intellectually independent, curious and honest is the man, (i.e., the more rational), the stronger will be his esthetic responses to things that less rational men might simply dismiss. I now point out that the esthetic response extends also to the observation of **the ideas and character traits of others**. It gives a man satisfaction to see other rational men **independently** have his ideas, reach his own conclusions, share his states of being. The more rational the man, and the closer the relationship, the greater the desire for this kind of relationship with others. In our closest personal relationships it might even be termed a "need". Some thinkers have called this relationship phenomenon "visibility", or "mirroring". Sadly, most rational men have little of this joy in their relationships, since rationality is so very rare.

As elsewhere in this Book, we contrast the rational man's emotional response to that of the irrational man. The irrational man too seeks some kind of "compatibility" in his close relationships, but in him it is "co-dependency".

The keen reader might notice that what I have described above as "mirroring" looks a bit like what we have elsewhere called intellectual dependency; and in fact, **in the hands of the irrational man, it is!** The irrational man too seeks out, for his relationships, others who share his ideas, his conclusions, his states of being. But, as pointed out, upon finding such people he experiences not satisfaction but **validation.** The two emotions are quite similar in their feeling – the difference being in their cause! The rational man conforms to nature while the irrational man attempts to conform nature to himself, and needs others to agree with him that he is "right".

THE GREATER LOVER AND THE LESSER LOVER

OUR BREATH COMES OUT WHITE CLOUDS,
MINGLES, AND HANGS IN THE AIR.
SPEAKING STRICTLY FOR ME,
WE BOTH COULD HAVE DIED THEN AND THERE.
Joan Baez
"Diamonds And Rust"

I hope that by now I have dispelled any automatic negative connotations regarding the concept of "power" in relationships. In the life of the rational man power is a beautiful thing. Power enables a man to pursue his goals and his heart's desires, and provide the heart's desires of those he loves and cares about. To be perfectly clear – in the lives of **rational** men, the more power, the better. The old adage regarding power is false: it is not power that corrupts man, but man's irrationality that corrupts power. I also hope I have made clear the role of "need" in love. It has been said by others that one cannot love what one needs. This is a conspiratorial, anti-self-esteem perpetration – and it is also a con.
(Before proceeding, let the reader thoroughly understand the points made on pages 82-84.)

A major obstacle to the proper understanding of love has been the prevailing attitude that one is entitled to what one needs. But we have solved that dilemma with the insight that one is **not** entitled to what one needs. Therefore, we are free to define love based on what it actually is **rather than as a reaction to our fears.** We boldly and unapologetically hold that one can ONLY love what, or who, one needs.

It was previously pointed out that, for various reasons, power is not evenly distributed among men. It is now pointed out that **need is also not evenly distributed among men.** In fact, in human relations, one man's "need" is another man's "power". With no "things or behaviors that men want or need" from one another, there is no power (as far as interpersonal relations go).

In her excellent two books on the man-woman relationship, Esther Vilar claims the opposite – that one person's **weaknesses** lead to their power in a relationship. Within the context of her books she was certainly correct! Our differing assessments lie in that her account was focused on a psychological interpretation which failed to consider all forms of want, need, and power at play in the man-woman relationship. She was not attempting to write a philosophy, but rather an account of male-female dynamics -- so she missed something and made the absurd assertion that the weaker person can be the more powerful one in a relationship. Therefore, to be exact, she was right about who generally has the power, but **incomplete as to why.** To fully explain the dynamics of any relationship all active forms of want, need, and power must be considered.

What all this means is that even in adequate relationships the partner with the greater need is in a position to **experience** the greater love, while the person with the lesser need generally experiences the greater power, and might have difficulty in maintaining his own love. Generally, the relationship **is more important to the greater lover** than it is to the lesser lover.

But the Greater Lover desperately wants to see love in the eyes of their beloved – he not only needs, but wants to **be needed.** If the Lesser Lover is unable to maintain adequate emotion he might tire of the Greater Lover's efforts. The Lesser Lover might experience self-conflict – wanting to be loved yet also come to envy the other's greater happiness. The Lesser Lover might take steps to sabotage the relationship. When faced with this, some possible strategies include, **1)** Accept the situation, **2)** the Lesser Lover might find a way to experience greater need, or **3)** the Lesser Lover might forgo some of his power. In the described situation no one is necessarily "wrong", but it would be heartless to ask the Greater Lover to give up some of his emotion when he is quite capable of experiencing it, (see "Make Me Feel Special", below).

If all relationships could be as benign as that described above then things might not be so bad. But, unfortunately, men often make things more difficult than they need be – much more difficult.

MISUSE OF POWER

> To speak about the Man/Woman Game it is necessary to
> distinguish it from the Boy/Girl Game. In the Boy/Girl Game
> when one person wants another the other is less likely to
> want back. In the Man/Woman Game when one person wants
> another the other is more likely to want back. In this Volume
> we do not deal with the Boy/Girl Game even though it is played
> by many adults. This Volume is about the Man/Woman Game.
> Ron Smothermon, M.D.
> The Man Woman Book

This Book is primarily about what works – which was my intention. However a few more words about what doesn't work are in order at this point.

To the extent that a man is irrational he may misuse power in his interactions with others. The misuse is basically of three forms, or some combination thereof – they are Force, Fraud and Manipulation. The man might use physical force in attempt to acquire the things or behaviors he wants from others. The man might fraudulently use the power of trade by breaking his promises and agreements. And finally, the man might abuse the intellectual power by taking advantage of the other's goodwill, character, gullibility or their needs. In close personal relationships that do not work, the issues broadly fit into two categories – "Bidding Up" and "Bidding Down".

"THE HARD BARGAINER" (Bidding Up)

This "accountant of relationships" (always the Lesser Lover) seeks great **material gain** from his powers, and frequently works hard on developing and maintaining his own powers to "up-bid" others. The Hard Bargainer may do his work both prior to, as well as during a relationship. He has a long list of qualities and behaviors required in another for a close relationship. The list goes well beyond his rational needs. The Hard Bargainer frequently manipulates and withholds, constantly on the lookout to coerce a better deal. The "society", in many cases, does bargaining on behalf of some group, thereby giving the **individual** Hard Bargainer **plausible deniability,** (for example, think back to the topic on Indentured Servitude). This type is likely to cause much pain and the ruination of families and lives. If men still lived primitively, with death or serious discomfort behind every tree, the Hard Bargainer might be becoming -- but in a free, romantic society of plenty, he is out of place. The only good thing to say about the Hard Bargainer is that they sometimes hurt themselves by ending up alone.

"MAKE ME FEEL SPECIAL"

Pay extremely close attention to this one, or you will miss it and think I'm even crazier than I am.

The Hard Bargainer is often practiced in its more twisted and suped-up form of "Make Me Feel Special". In this variation, the Lesser Lover wants to **feel, or function as the Greater Lover** on a more-or-less permanent basis, as well as to **appear** to be the Greater Lover to those outside the relationship,,,,, BUT,,,,,, the Lesser Lover is actually in the position of power and privilege in the relationship, **and would never give that up.** This requires the person **who is actually the greater lover** to perfect a "tough, play it cool" act, both as a show to the world, as well a façade between the couple – a façade that never lasts. The Greater Lover develops the skill of suppressing or hiding his enjoyment of life, and, in particular, his enjoyment of relationships; for he must never appear to be happier than the pretending Lesser Lover. If the Greater Lover ever blows his cover the relationship is probably in trouble, which of course almost always happens. This game takes a great deal of intellectual and emotional energy on the part of the Greater Lover, and there are many who try to play it, and many who demand it.

"THE BULLDOZER" (Bidding Down)

Sometimes a person (usually the Lesser Lover) is unhappy with promises he made to secure the relationship. Previously we pointed out that all relationship problems (as relationship problems) are some kind of power struggle or misuse of power. The Bulldozer has a shorter "list" than the previously discussed Hard Bargainer, but makes up for it in the misery caused. The Bulldozer usually starts out in a somewhat weaker bargaining position, and so, unlike the Hard Bargainer, is forced to do his work only AFTER the relationship is established. The Bulldozer wishes to break the promises he made to secure his relationship and "bulldoze" a new agreement onto the other. The Bulldozer might think, "What is the minimum that I can put into this relationship and still keep it?". The Bulldozer will frequently **reduce their standards** for themselves or the relationship to "down-bid" the other. The Bulldozer never picks a power struggle he cannot win. The Bulldozer is not so much interested in love as in getting by at a bargain price, and causes great pain for the Greater Lover. In fact, the only limit to the Bulldozer's ability to cause pain is the limit of his power (i.e., the other's need). As usual the Greater Lover simply suffers or the relationship ends in destruction; often the destruction of a whole family and the ruination of lives.

"POUND OF FLESH"

A version of bidding down that deserves special mention is "Pound Of Flesh". Frequently one knows couples who have been together for quite some time and appear happy together, however, one of the pair (usually the Lesser Lover) might casually say, "Yes we are happy now, but a long time ago we went

90

through some trouble that we had to work through.", or something like that. If one listens very carefully he might even hear just a tinge of satisfaction or pride in the statement, as if he had gotten away with something – which is exactly what happened. If two people can be happy together now then why did they ever need to be unhappy? Here is an explanation of what happened:

The Greater Lover would share anything, do almost anything for love. But there is one possession, his most precious possession, that cannot be shared – his own happiness. The Lesser Lover sees the great happiness of the other, covets it, and responds with envy. Even while claiming to love, the lesser lover begins, with mathematical precision, to withhold everything that the Greater Lover loved for. The Greater Lover desperately tries to hold on and when the withholding fails to destroy his love, perpetrations are begun by the Lesser Lover.

Now there are two serious problems where before there was only one – the Greater Lover's love and trust has now been deeply damaged. Sometimes couples will break up over this sickness. Occasionally the Lesser Lover can be helped, although the relationship will never be the same. Usually the Lesser Lover extracts enough pain, or compliance with demands, or broken dreams, to satisfy his envy and they continue on – the Greater Lover spending the years covering up the scar across his dreams. In how many relationships does this happen?

It is challenges such as these that even the best of men frequently face. Close personal relationships can only be satisfying between rational people. People are individuals who must have the freedom to fully exercise all of their powers as they see fit, to work out the best life for themselves that they can. That is probably the greatest relationship need of all!

WHEN THE WANT OF LOVE OVERCOMES THE LOVE OF POWER,
THE WORLD WILL KNOW PEACE.
Jimmy Hendrix

MOTIVATING RELATIONSHIP

I have described that love is the emotional **reward** for the effort of achieving a needs-meeting relationship. I have also described that man does nothing unless he is motivated to do it, and that emotions perform this function also. So, what is the **motivating emotion** for relationship? Society already has the emotion identified, albeit disparagingly, so we will have to **re-habilitate** it – it is called **infatuation!**

When one person meets another, and senses the possibility of a desirable relationship, he will need to be **motivated to do things** to develop that relationship. He risks time and disappointment in pursuing that relationship. He may even give certain material things with no guarantee that his efforts will be reciprocated. If the relationship is to be a very close one, and a good one, each person will likely need to give certain important things as tokens of their hope and good will -- **still not certain** that an ongoing relationship has been established. (Needless to say, tokens received should be sincere **and not mere attempts at manipulation by the other.** The hopeful lover risks this too!) To accomplish these things will require motivation. Therefore, prior to the establishment of a relationship a relatively short period of "false love" is appropriate, and necessary! The emotion is not to be called love just yet, as an ongoing needs-meeting relationship has not been established; so the emotion is given its own name – infatuation. The emotion feels like love, and is frequently more intense than the real long-term thing. But this Book was written partly to help men enhance the real long-term thing!

The above completes the description of what infatuation is, and its purpose. However, it would be an omission to not discuss just how infatuation got its somewhat negative connotation!

First, the obvious. I discussed previously how people bring to relationships both their personal, as well as interpersonal, problems. Clearly, the infatuated person can hang on to a hopeful relationship long after it should be clear that it will not happen. The infatuated person might annoy their love interest or even cause them problems. Since neither power nor rationality are evenly distributed among men, it is understandable how some people might feel and behave in less than optimal ways. When people disparage infatuation it is generally this type of thing that they are referring to. However, that is not the whole story!

I pointed out that all relationship problems (as relationship problems) ultimately reduce to some abuse, misuse, or unwise use of power. The problems with infatuation **can also reside within the object of infatuation!** The period of infatuation can be artificially extended by the "beloved" for weeks, months or years, by the **promise** of a relationship which may, or may not, happen. This may be done by the person of greater power in order to reduce their own risks, keep their options open, extract more concessions and promises, or boost a false sense of self-esteem. This feature of relationships is built into the current **socio-**

92

political fabric and frequently is a significant contributing factor in the behavior of the infatuated person. When the period of infatuation is dragged on by the "lover", he is rightfully held responsible, yet when it is dragged on by the "love object", responsibility is rarely levied. The bottom line is that as the period before "just getting on with the relationship" keeps getting extended, it is likely that there are trust and/or power issues at work.

SUMMARY OF POLITICS
1) Men are social beings in that they have a general, albeit varying interest in one another. This is the origin of the field of politics.
2) Men's interest in one another is caused by the "things and behaviors that men want and need" from one another.
3) Politics is the study of the proper rules of all social interaction.
4) The ways that men acquire the things and behaviors that they want and need is called "power". There are three forms of power:
   a) Intellectual Power – the power of knowledge, wisdom and persuasion
   b) Economic Power -- the power of all production and material trade
   c) Physical Force
5) It is desirable to eliminate the power of Physical Force from human relationships. This is because of man's unique nature, which is different from other animals.
6) The field of politics is the study of why all human interactions should be voluntary – eliminating physical force to the extent practical and leaving men free to exercise their intellectual and economic powers.

When you finally do come to see
The things you wanted on your plate,
Were being provided by little me
Through that thing you lovingly call the state,
And you also find it was all a scam -
Remember these words that wise man spake:
"You just can't cheat an honest man".
The Author

PART 5: SOME TOPICS AND CONSIDERATIONS

Since this Book is about philosophy, and since philosophy is the organizing field for all human thought, I offer this Part as a **sampling** of Topics. Given time I could think of any number of additional illustrative examples to discuss. These topics are presented in the spirit of illustrating the reasoning process and Intellectual Curiosity. So let's see how the ideas discussed in this Book apply to some everyday issues.

THE HIGHER AND THE LOWER

It should be clear by now that the rational world is a completely different place than the irrational. The world in which we live is designed by, and for, the irrational – to serve their wants and make their lives bearable. The toll of this continued state of affairs on human life is immense, but only the rational is aware of the full scale of it. The irrational struggles to see the glass as half full, while the rational clearly sees it as half empty. The irrational does not understand the rational. It is as if the rational lives atop a beautiful mesa. The rational looks down upon the plains below and sees and understands, but the irrational does not see.

THE CAUSE OF EVIL AND OTHER MENTAL SICKNESS

HOW IS IT THAT MEN KNOW WHAT IS GOOD
YET DO WHAT IS BAD?

Socrates

The expression of the Primary Vices and Virtues in society is like the old **house of distorted mirrors** at a carnival – nothing is as it seems. When moral distinction is made between them it is usually to disparage the Primary Virtues. Intellectual dependence, expressed as collectivism, is highly valued. The collectivist is seen as a member, a team player, useful; while the intellectually independent man – an eccentric, a trouble maker, of little use or even a threat to be shunned or eliminated. Intellectual Curiosity (except in one's chosen career or hobbies) is seen as little more than a personal choice, another hobby, optional. Praise of this virtue is reserved primarily for the great thinkers who have advanced man's technology to increase man's entertainment, comfort, luxury or self-pride -- but little (praise), if any, for the regular man who only wants to understand life and be rational. Intellectual dullness or laziness is considered perfectly fine if one can get away with it by being popular, rich, powerful, or good looking enough. The intellectually honest man is seen as obstinate, uncompromising, un-cooperative, a dreamer; while the intellectually dishonest man is "flexible" – someone who can "work with others" and make it in the "real world", someone who believes "what we believe".

A man making mistakes in trying to practice the Primary Virtues is punished, while the man of the Primary Vices is given a pass, or even rewarded. The end result of this state is that men attempt to practice **derivative** virtues without practicing the **primary** ones -- they attempt to avoid evil while practicing vice! This was noticed too by E.F. Schumacher, who described it thus:

> "Anyone who goes openly into a journey to the interior, who withdraws from the ceaseless agitation of daily life and pursues the kind of training ,,,,,,,, without which genuine self-knowledge cannot be obtained, is accused of selfishness and of turning his back on his social duties. Meanwhile, world crises multiply and everybody deplores the shortage, or even total lack, of wise men, unselfish leaders, trustworthy counselors, etc."

For all my adult life I have asked myself why men do bad things that lead to tragedy. At length, a breakthrough occurred for me that no fact comes forth as the single cause of evil, but rather **four things,** one or another of which usually seemed to **predominate in any one particular man.** They were: **1)** The man was following a crowd, just doing what others did or, **2)** The man didn't know any better -- he was ill informed about the facts of a case, yet did something anyway or, **3)** The man was indeed informed (in a sense), believed himself to be doing good, yet still committed acts that led to harm or, **4)** The man was openly dishonest and knowingly committed evil acts.

In the above paragraph, the openly dishonest man is by far the **least common** yet the **only one** generally considered evil by polite society! The discussion in the first two paragraphs of this Topic illustrates why this is so -- men wish to have their cake and eat it too! Items 1 through 3 above are clearly nothing but the expression of the Primary Vices! There is a conspiracy to not condemn the Primary Vices, **but only their results!** (Once again, the "Problem Oriented Thinking" from Page F-7!). This is not to say that openly dishonest men aren't evil - they are - but is to say that such men are society's scapegoats, taking the blame **for what almost everyone else is up to!** The fact is that the relatively few openly evil men could little function without the aid and comfort of the masses practicing the Primary Vices! This is why evil never dies away – **it is NEVER actually fought!**

We see now why evil has been so elusive and sneaky. It is at once a social problem that can be solved only by individual perseverance, or to put the matter another way, an individual problem that can be easily passed off as a social one.

Most commonly, the evil man is unaware that he is evil, and in fact thinks he is good. The premise of this Book, however, is that he is still accountable for his actions. All evil must be paid for by someone and **justice** requires that it be paid by the man who committed the error and not by the man who did not. Much law and custom in society is for the purpose of spreading the results of evil or outright transferring those results to the good! The great injustices in the World are not primarily against the billions of men who's dominant mental state is the Primary Vices but against the relatively few men who practice the Primary Virtues. Every man who does live rationally and prospers did so by his own efforts, and could have chosen otherwise -- the man, therefore, deserves the fruits of his efforts. The less rational man tends to underestimate the efforts and struggles of rational men. Furthermore, any misfortunes befallen to less rational men are not the fault of the rational man and, though he may indeed choose to help others, he must not be forced to.

> ONLY SAYING THAT WE WILL DO BETTER NEXT TIME
> GUARANTEES THAT THERE WILL BE A NEXT TIME.
> Unknown

The virtuous man retains the right to exercise all of his powers. Under a government there are likely to be, so called, "victimless crime" laws which are intended to control a man's life or take his property should he break such laws. The breaking of, or compliance with, such laws is at the discretion of the virtuous man, and, in fact, he should break such laws at his convenience – and do it proudly! The virtuous man harms no one by exercising his Economic or Intellectual powers.

Evil in a society is like a cancer – in the beginning is starts out as wrong ideas. Wrong ideas are attractive because they seem to offer (in the short term) easy ways out of man's problems. Try to correct men holding these wrong ideas and what one gets from them is something like, "I haven't hurt anyone. It's a free country isn't it? I have the right to my opinions. Who are you to teach me anything? Mind your own business." Then the ideas spread and become held by enough people that actions are taken on the ideas. By then it is too late -- the horse is out of the barn and cannot be put back in -- those holding the evil ideas and principles are in control.

We are now down to the very root of things and can see why the cause of evil is simply "irrationality", i.e., having the **Primary Vices** as one's dominant mental states. To repeat the earlier crucial observation - each of the Virtues is a separate mental state for dealing with the three fundamental existents which all men must face; **1)** the minds of other men, **2)** the whole of nature herself, and **3)** his own mind. These are the sources of all evil and good.

Earlier I claimed that "The Rocky Horror Show" was a story of warning – the **theme** of the play being "the spread of evil". I also said that Americans were not a particularly philosophical lot. It is thus that in the **U.S. movie version** of the play the most crucial lines at the end of the story were removed. Here are the words that were removed because they were deemed too serious for the American audience:

"SUPER HEROES"

I've done a lot
God knows I've tried
To find the truth
I've even lied
But all I know
Is down inside I'm bleeding

And Super Heroes
Come to feast
To taste the flesh
Not yet deceased
And all I know
Is still the beast is feeding

THE HAPPINESS EQUATION

This Book has been about achieving one's true happiness in ourselves and in relation to others. When we look closely at ourselves, or at other men, to estimate the presence of this condition we call "happiness", we see that in addition to happiness are also attempts to mask unhappiness, or **intellectual pain.** A man wants to be happy and when he cannot achieve it by proper human means he will attempt to **fake it,** both for himself as well as before others in a social setting -- as an obviously unhappy man is generally not very popular. The man acquires certain attitudes and behaviors which temporarily alleviate his pain and pass it off for happiness.

There are basically two types of attitudes/behaviors that men develop to mask their intellectual pain, and without further ado I present to the reader, for his consideration, what I call the **Happiness Equation:**

$$\text{Apparent Happiness} = \text{Real Happiness} + \text{"Self" Destructive Behaviors (Addictions)} + \text{"Other" Destructive Behaviors (Perpetrations)}$$

The above diagram says that when we look at ourselves, or other men, we actually see a combination of real happiness **and** attempts to mask intellectual pain. The person attempts to pass off the destructive behavior as real happiness. This can work for a time, particularly if the destructive behavior is **socially acceptable.** However, if the man is prohibited the destructive behaviors the extent of his real happiness comes crashing in on him. In some cases there is very little real happiness in the man.

The, so called, **self**-destructive behaviors consist of a number of things but are primarily a man's addictive tendencies. Addictions are the "fillers and pain killers" of life. It is important to emphasize that the "destruction" of addiction refers **equally to the destruction or stunting of man's intellect** as to his physical existence. Addiction, as in most other of man's problems, is primarily an

99

intellectual matter. The **other**-destructive behaviors are primarily the various perpetrations against others in which men engage. Virtually any activity can be engaged "as an addiction", and this is indeed how many men pursue much of their daily life. One example of men's perpetrations is racism. An example of something that can be both addiction and perpetration would be gossip. The general pattern is for men to move about their day from one destructive behavior to another, sometimes spending very little of their time in real happiness. Men try to keep their destructive behaviors among those that are socially acceptable, but often fail in this. A man will never give up his destructive behaviors unless he can decrease his intellectual pain and increase his Real Happiness -- so I wrote this Book.

Another aspect of the present topic is that men can have truly meaningful personal relationships only **to the extent of their real happiness,** however, this is often lacking in men. So men attempt to fake happiness in the relationship too by making their addictions and perpetrations **a feature of the relationship.** This requires seeking out relationship partners with the same, or complimentary, addictions and perpetrations. The psychology field even has a term for this – it's called "co-dependency" -- and is, to some degree, a feature of almost every relationship.

POLARIZATION
(I don't care what your argument is because I don't have to)

WHAT A FIELD DAY FOR THE HEAT
A THOUSAND PEOPLE IN THE STREET
SINGIN' SONGS AND A-CARRYIN' SIGNS
MOSTLY SAY "HOORAY FOR OUR SIDE"
"For What It's Worth"
Stephen Stills

The intellectually independent man who stands on his own two feet cannot afford to be wrong. He makes it his business to know what he is doing. The buck stops with him. As such, the independent man listens to what others have to say and learns from them when appropriate. He readily gives up his position on any matter when a better position comes along. He is constantly on the lookout for better ideas.

But the intellectually dependent man (the collectivist) is in the opposite position. The collectivist man **can** afford to be wrong (in the short term) because

100

he has his "in-group" to prop him up, to tell him he is right, to fight for his cause, to defend him from rival groups, to persecute others – to fight his wars.

As such, we see in society that most issues which have a moral bearing are **polarized.** The defining characteristics of polarized issues are that at least one side, often both, does not listen to the arguments of the other. At least one of the sides, often both, has an agenda that is more important than truth. Frequently the issue itself is merely a pawn in some larger goal of one side, or both. Frequently one side of the issue is actually correct, though they might not fully understand **why** they are correct. It's as if they are right simply by the luck of being within that particular in-group. But, as the man who has been reading this Book now understands, this is not "being right" at all. A man must know **why** he is right. It is well known in the science community that one does not get credit for just guessing – the scientist must have an understanding of why something is so. If men think that science and technology will save us, then let men apply the **methods** of science to understanding life.

One good example of polarization is our polarized politics of government – memorialized by the "two party system". This system is certainly held in place by the attitudes of most voters, but there are also certain laws which exist to ensure its perpetuation. There are any number of ways of **tweaking election systems** to favor a two party system. The majority of voters in each side have agendas not wholly consistent with freedom and depend on opposition of the other side to prevent loss of power, exposure of hypocrisies and contradictions, etc. – and **viable** alternative parties would upset this balance. The small fraction of voters (and it IS a small fraction) who really "get it" have nowhere to go. Rather than being a force for good, the two party political system has been a significant factor in our demise – it protects the status quo – and most voters **like it that way,** their complaints to the contrary!

The bottom line of this Topic is that everything that men need to know has already been said or written – it's just that no one is listening. So, another purpose of this Book is to allow the reader to give up polarization.

> I DO NOT KNOW, AND CANNOT IMAGINE, ANY GROUP
> WHICH DOES NOT INCLUDE AMONG ITS IDEAS AN
> ENORMOUS DOSE OF LIES. THAT BEING THE CASE,
> THE ALTERNATIVE IS INEVITABLE:
> EITHER ONE MUST LIKE FALSEHOOD,
> OR ONE MUST DISLIKE THE FAMILIAR SETTINGS
> OF DAILY LIFE.
> Yves Simon

"PARENTAL AUTHORITY"

CHILDREN ARE SPECIAL BECAUSE OF WHO THEY ARE,
NOT WHO'S THEY ARE.
                                                    Ron Smothermon, M.D.

One sometimes hears, correctly I think, that one source of the plight of children is their own caretakers failure to exercise "authority". Let us go back and consider authority from the beginning, for before a man can exercise such a quality he must first possess it.

Before proceeding it must be made clear the nature of the caretaker-protégé relationship. It was observed previously that the **origin** of any consequential human interaction are the "things and behaviors that men want and need from one another". The caretaker-protégé relationship is no different and is subject to the same principles governing all human interactions – but with one exception. The relationship concerns the starting of a new human life and the protégé does not ask to be born into this world – that decision is made by **one parent.** Consequently the protégé is powerless and is **entitled** to certain things -- but only in the sense that the caretaker cares for the protégé not by right, but by privilege. If the caretaker is unable or unwilling to meet certain needs of the protégé, he may lose the privilege. Obviously, in a civilized society there would be lawful ways of dealing with that eventuality. The protégé has a broad spectrum of needs, while the needs of the caretaker are narrow and should be primarily intellectual. However, the caretaker is **entitled to nothing from the protégé, as in all other human relationships.**

We have shown that, ultimately, all good things spring forth from a man's rationality. Or, to put the point negatively, to the extent that a man is not rational, good things come to him **in spite of his irrationality** and not because of it. We have shown that a man's rationality begins with the Primary Virtues and all their derivative virtues. We have shown that the practice of a man's virtues leads, other things being equal, to his Powers (economic and intellectual). And finally we have shown that a man uses his powers to pursue and achieve his goals, and then the man chooses to be happy. If the reader is under the impression that "authority" is a quality one possesses simply by virtue of **being a caretaker,** or by being bigger, or stronger, or older, or even "smarter" than another, then he is tragically mistaken. On the contrary, the only source of any man's authority is his

102

rationality, which means his Virtues and his Powers. Therefore, let us consider how the Virtues and Powers stack up for the caretaker in relation to their protégés.

Consider the Primary Virtues. The newborn child clearly comes into the world with perfect Intellectual Independence. The new born child doesn't care one whit about what other people think about anything. Of course the child has an **instinct** for mimicking or copying the actions and mannerisms of those around it, but this is hardly the collectivism which will be imposed upon him later. As soon as the child begins to acquire a **mind** of his own, he will attempt to assert independence, **(i.e., conformance with reality as he sees it),** other things being equal. Likewise for the virtues of Intellectual Curiosity and Honesty. The evidence is that children's brains have an inherent curiosity and general unwillingness to hold contradictions. Once again, the vices of intellectual dullness and dishonesty are learned later on. Therefore, we see that in every case children enter the world **superior to their caretakers in the Primary Virtues!** As far as the Primary Virtues are concerned the caretaker has nothing positive to offer the protégé – the protégé is an expert in them. The caretaker can only hope to have some influence in the **derivative** virtues, if the caretaker has any. As always, it is the example that the caretaker sets which counts – actions speak much louder than words.

There is a movie called "The Family Man" with a touching illustration of the Primary Virtues in children. In the plot, a man is temporarily assigned by the powers-that-be to a different life in which he has a family – yet he retains his existing self. Obviously out of place, his little girl of about five, after some observation, calmly says "You're not my daddy." Having fessed up to the little girl, she gives assistance to him in getting by (it's their little secret). Of note is how the little girl is intellectually independent – "I can handle this myself." -- she doesn't go and tell mommy. She is intellectually honest – he is not her daddy,,,,,but he **looks** like her daddy, and he seems nice enough. And finally, her participation in the ruse is driven by her innocent curiosity – "Let's see where this goes!". In the moving climax the man comes to accept and love his new role -- the **girl now fooled by his love** into thinking that her daddy has returned! It is true that we could never test the reality of this scenario -- nor would most five year-olds behave this calmly if the situation could be replicated. However,

103

children much younger than five do tend to "take life as it comes", as the little girl in the movie – something we should all do more of. This plot element in the movie is an example of "idealization of human character traits" in art, mentioned previously in this Book. Such idealizations are done by the creators of art to illustrate truths.

CHILDREN CAN DEAL WITH THE WAY IT IS
IF THEY CAN FIND OUT THE WAY IT IS.
ADULTS SPEND MUCH EFFORT PRETENDING
ABOUT LIFE AND THIS IS CONFUSING FOR CHILDREN.
Ron Smothermon, M.D.

Let us now turn to the Powers - Economic and Intellectual. Remember that "economics" deals with far more than merely money – in our context it concerns a man's entire relationship to his material life. Does the man "own things", or do things "own him"? What about that big house in the fancy neighborhood? Can he easily afford it, or are both caretakers working their asses off, leaving little time for the little ones? How about those credit cards? Are they maxed out? In a man's job, is he honest, or does he "play the game" to "get ahead"? Does the man guiltily buy his protégé's love and affection with gifts, or does he allow the child to exercise creativity and learn the joy of anticipation and the value of earning things for himself? These, and many other things, determine a man's economic power. If the caretaker lacks real Economic Power he will fail the protégé in his relationship to his material existence.

Next we turn to the Intellectual Power. Of course children copy, and do have a natural Intellectual Curiosity, but their intellectual power is still only a **potential,** not an actuality. If their caretakers are intellectually dull the protégé will likely copy that style of thinking, and learning new things will become an increasingly difficult task. If the caretakers are not very conceptual then the protégé will likely acquire that character trait. Is the caretaker a faithful reader? (not to the protégé but for his own pleasure!!) What does the caretaker read? This is important. Does the caretaker have a sincere interest in new and interesting ideas? Is the caretaker "open minded" in the best sense of that term? Does the caretaker lead an intellectual life, or avoid thinking deeply as best he can? Does the caretaker exhibit all manner of addictions before the protégé? A man can be addicted to virtually any thing or situation! One cannot nourish in another what one does not have himself.

104

Finally we consider the issue of Physical Force. Children are born with no mental **content** and can easily get into trouble if left to their own devices. I leave it to the reader to consider the cases and manners in which some kind of physical force might be appropriate for the protection of children. However, all too often, the general pattern is to lean on physical force as a general solution due to **deficiency** in the other powers of the caretaker. If all one has is a hammer, all problems are nails.

> AND SO IT HAPPENS THAT THE PATHS OF CHILDREN
> CROSS WITH THOSE OF ADULTS IN ONE HUNDRED PLACES
> EVERY DAY. THEY NEVER GO IN THE SAME DIRECTION,
> NOR TO THEY REST ON THE SAME FOUNDATION.
>
> Robert Louis Stevenson, "Child's Play"
> From: Freedom: The End Of The Human Condition
> Jeremy Griffith

In closing, it is emphasized that even a caretaker with excellent authority and the skill to exercise it is fighting a hard battle with the irrational world in which we live, which offers young people short-term, easy ways out. Each caretaker has his own personality and "style" in exercising what authority he does possess, and some styles simply work better than others. And lastly, each child has his own free will (of thought) and so, ultimately, makes of the world around him what he will. The bottom line is that the greatest gift a caretaker can give the protégé is the message that **life is intelligible and can be understood and lived.**

POVERTY

> A MAN MAY OWN A THOUSAND ACRES
> YET HE SLEEPS ON A BED OF FIVE FEET.
> Chinese Proverb
>
> SOME PEOPLE ARE SO POOR ALL THEY HAVE IS MONEY.
> Patrick Meagher

Prior to discussing poverty it is necessary to dispense with several false notions regarding it which render clear thinking on the matter impossible.

The first is that prior to any discussion of poverty there must be agreement between parties as to what constitutes a **free society;** for in an un-free society nothing is possible (ultimately) **except oppression and widespread, unrelenting poverty.** It has been made clear in this Volume what a free society is, and any disagreement as to its importance and desirability thereby ends any discussion regarding poverty.

105

Secondly, there are children, handicapped and elderly people who live in quite unfortunate conditions, yet this too cannot be what is meant by "poverty". Children are under the charge of their designated caretakers who have every opportunity to meet their charges' needs **in a free society.** The elderly, **living in a free society,** had every opportunity in their younger years to develop family and other relationships, as well as their intellectual and economic powers to care for themselves in their golden years. Turning to the handicapped – **in a free society** this class of people in need will be a small factor to be dealt with by voluntary charity. I stipulated in the Forward to this Volume that a philosophy cannot be built upon special or emergency cases, of which charity cases are an example. Therefore, though we may have a discussion about the handicapped, the potential plight of the handicapped also cannot be what is meant by "poverty".

Stripped of the above obfuscating issues we are simply left with poverty as **the practice of Vice in man's life** (the Primary Vices and their derivative vices)! In a free society the only factors which can cause a man failure is the practice of Vice and, of course, plain bad luck.

In a free society the practice of the Primary Virtues (and their derivative virtues) will gain for a man his powers (economic and intellectual). Then, other things being equal, the practice of his powers will allow a man to achieve his goals.

It is important to understand that, in a similar manner to the concept of "economics", the concept of "poverty" encompasses the whole of a man's relationship to his intellectual as well as his material life. This stands in contrast to the prevailing attitude that poverty is primarily "a lack of material goods". (I am fully aware that the do-gooders and busybodies in society pay lip service to the "whole man" in their proselytizing on poverty -- yet the results of their actions do not bear this out.) The **virtuous man in a free society** is rich, rich, rich, regardless of his particular station in life, while the man of vice is poor, poor, poor, though he may be "filthy rich".

A great deal has been said and written regarding poverty. As caring human beings we all wish poverty to end and know that our lives are lesser for its existence. Poverty is a tremendous drain on human life as well as on the Earth itself, for poverty is the primary factor in the human **population explosion,** which is, in turn, the greatest single material threat to man's civilized and comfortable way of life. In a sense **this entire Volume** has been nothing but an instruction manual on how to end poverty.

HOW DOES ONE IMPROVE ONE'S CONCEPTUAL THINKING

A PROBLEM IS NOT TO BE SOLVED FROM
THE SAME MENTALITY THAT CREATED IT.
Albert Einstein

We compare the conceptual structure of the **rational** man's mind/brain to a "brick wall". In such a conceptual structure there might be errors in thinking, yet the man can safely remove any brick found to be misplaced and correct the mistake, thereby making the entire structure even more sound. Then too, we compare the conceptual structure of the highly irrational man to a "house of cards". In this conceptual structure the adjustment of any of the many misplaced cards threatens to bring down the entire structure. This is why the irrational man will not listen – **any unfamiliar fact or idea, whether true or false!,** is a threat to him! To quote, again, Philip Wylie:

> Illusion,,,,,as the basis of man's usual image means
> that to be **un-deceived** in any one way, however small,
> threatens the sum of all delusions. (emphasis mine)
>
> Philip Wylie
> The Magic Animal

One of my purposes in writing this Book is to give support and encouragement to those reading it in their quest for better thinking and better lives. It all begins with one's **intentions.** Intention here is the **stand** that, **1)** Life makes sense and is perfect, **2)** That only man creates confusion and unnecessary suffering, and **3)** That a man will do **whatever it takes** to acquire the skills to make his life work – that he will search to the ends of the Earth for whatever he needs to succeed. This must be one's dedication.

Then, the quest continues by practicing the Primary Virtues. Earlier I stated that if a man **actually practices** the Primary Virtues, then he will be rational. I think that one may begin with what one is most comfortable with. If one is particularly fearful of the opinions of others, he might begin **privately** by working on his factual knowledge and understanding (Intellectual Curiosity) and getting things straight in his own mind (Intellectual Honesty). But, I'm sorry to say, eventually the piper will have to be paid and the thinking man will have to assert his Intellectual Independence as well. All of the virtues must ultimately be practiced as a unity or none will be practiced well.

A man must develop the conscious habit of being observant -- of **noticing things.** A man's conceptual structure is built upon the similarities and differences between the things and ideas of which he is aware. The richness and depth of a man's rationality is limited by how skillful he is at noticing these similarities and differences. This is a skill that can be improved.

And finally, a man must take concepts seriously. Although ideas are not material things they are still real, and he must take "clashes between ideas" (i.e., contradictions) to be as **serious** as clashes between material things – like car crashes. In other words, for the rational man, ideas are real and important.

THE EDUCATION SYSTEM (Some Observations)

SOME CAREFUL OBSERVERS HAVE EXPRESSED THE
QUITE HONEST CONVICTION THAT UNLESS THOUGHT
BE RAISED TO A FAR HIGHER PLAIN THAN HITHERTO,
SOME GREAT SET-BACK TO CIVILIZATION IS INEVITABLE.

> James Harvey Robinson
> From: The Importance Of Living
> Lin Yutang

I BELIEVE THAT OUR ABILITY TO COPE WITH
THE GREAT CRISES THAT LIE AHEAD WILL
DEPEND UPON OUR ABILITY TO RECAPTURE
THAT LOST ART OF LEARNING.

> Barry Goldwater
> The Conscience Of A Conservative

I at one time considered teaching as a career, but even had I acquired excellent teaching skills per se, I likely would have been a poor fit for the educational system as currently constituted. The situation is very unfortunate and it is difficult to tell whether things would have to be as they are in every way. One of the more well-meaning yet devastating problems I see is the temptation to push ever larger amounts of information onto students at younger and younger ages, at the expense of giving less information but with a deeper understanding of the subjects. For example, good science students may be able to recite that Rontgen discovered X-rays, yet not understand the significance of that fact. (Answer: It was not that doctors could now see broken bones. When the rays were investigated they were found to be "light" rays – the first discovery of "light"

108

other than visible light - a profound insight at the time. Even most science teachers do not get this. People had always felt the "heat" from fires and hot objects, but had no idea that this too was light.) Likewise, students are taught the word "energy", yet have little understanding of what, or how precious a resource, it is.

Not only has our modern complex world accelerated this "cramming" trend, but it is also the only way that many people now think and learn! Students come to school unable to follow a line of reasoning – "Just show us how to work the problems." The result is a world of educated idiots, or at best specialists, with men who actually understand the "big picture" few and far between. For students retaining virtue of Intellectual Curiosity such cramming of information during their school years would be less necessary, leaving more time for deeper discussion. The cramming is practiced by the educational system on the (correct) assumption that few people continue meaningful learning after their formal education. As man's store of knowledge becomes ever more complex, general education should contain **less** cramming and **more** explaining! We are moving in the opposite direction from which we should be. But still, it all begins in the home; schools cannot fix what is already broken.

Another issue I see seems to be the overuse of multiple choice answers on tests. There are cases where this method might be appropriate, and even necessary for logistical purposes, such as for standardized testing -- but as a normal method of testing seems like a bad idea. Students should learn to **search their entire field of knowledge and understanding** when solving a problem or demonstrating their intellectual competency.

I make these brief observations on education in full awareness of the other massive problems and evils seen in the educational system, obvious to any rational man. Many, but certainly not all, of such problems have been caused by the usurping of the educational function by the State.

THE OBJECT OF TRUE EDUCATION IS TO MAKE MEN NOT MERELY
DO THE RIGHT THINGS BUT ENJOY THE RIGHT THINGS,
NOT MERELY LEARNED BUT LOVE KNOWLEDGE,
NOT MERELY INDUSTRIOUS BUT LOVE INDUSTRY,
NOT MERELY PURE BUT LOVE PURITY,
NOT MERELY JUST BUT HUNGER AND THIRST FOR JUSTICE.
John Ruskin

OBSESSION WITH EMOTIONS AND POWER

Emotions and power are means to ends rather than the ends themselves. It was pointed out that, in a superficial sense, we do engage in our actions in pursuit of pleasant emotions, but that the rational man mindful that it is our RATIONAL life and actions that produce happiness and not simply the pursuit of emotions. One will never be happy simply by "trying to be happy" – it's **cause must be enacted.** The motivation to be happy and the reward of happiness must be intervened by a thought process and not simply connected by an action.

Likewise, a man can become obsessed with power (force, economic, intellectual), as if the mere possession of power, and the material things it can command, caused happiness. Remember that power is how men acquire the "things and behaviors that men want and need". The more power one has, the more things and behaviors one can potentially secure. It is easy to become trapped in this fact and lose sight of the source of one's power and happiness – one's rationality. In a free society the use of force is banned and men must acquire the things they want by their own efforts, and by trade or persuasion. The rational man has needs and his wants are carefully selected – the opposite of arbitrary – and are not unlimited. In a free society it is easy for the rational man to have more power than needed to meet his heart's desires. Only the rational man can experience what corrupt politicians have termed "freedom from want".

WHY DON'T PEOPLE JUST LISTEN TO REASON,
(and get smart the easy way)?

Everyone wants to be rational – if it doesn't cost anything. The fact is that it **doesn't** cost anything **in the long run**. The man who has largely achieved rationality would not trade it for anything, and considers the efforts along the way to have been worth it. It is these "efforts along the way" that are the problem for most men.

What are these efforts? It's quite simple you see. One goes out of agreement with the irrational world when exercising his Intellectual Independence; one struggles to overcome his intellectual dullness and lethargy to gain the necessary new knowledge; and Intellectual Honesty with oneself is difficult and painful, particularly at first. When exercising one's Intellectual

110

Independence it can be difficult to find others who will happily play the game of life with oneself. One will be misunderstood. One will make mistakes. To exercise Intellectual Curiosity, what does one read? Where does one find it? Whom should one listen to? Who is telling the truth and how does one tell? How does one exercise Intellectual Honesty? It is frightening to jettison cherished notions that one has known all of one's life and replace them with promising leads that, nevertheless, remain to be personally validated. How does one start? How far back to go? One cannot become a child again – rather, one must work within one's existing concept structure.

Man is a conceptual thinker. Regardless of how deficient or erroneous his concept structure is, it is still there. For the irrational man his concepts are like the proverbial "house of cards". He intuitively knows that the acceptance of even the simplest new fact could collapse his concept structure. Then too, to accept the new fact might require an immense amount of work to shore up his mental stability – deciding which new knowledge to accept, what existing good knowledge to keep, which existing ideas are false – all to improve a brain-mind that is serving him adequately for now, **though probably at expense to others**,,,,,, so why change?

So the irrational man doesn't listen. In fact, the more important the message the less the irrational man listens. There is, however, one instance when the irrational man will listen – when one is speaking in his cliché's, for he loves to hear how right he is. The cliché's are like little pieces of people's concept structures, **little viruses that float about society** within people's "in-groups". But these viruses are the opposite of ordinary viruses. Rather than infecting their hosts these viruses provide a continuing immunity – **immunity from change.**

But the rational man is in a different position. His concept structure is more like the brick wall. He can tolerate finding a mis-laid brick now and then, remove it and re-set it without fear of collapse. The rational man **wants** to find mis-laid bricks!

But there is another reason why the irrational man won't listen -- he can't believe that another man might actually have solved some problem within the humanities. How could he think so? Interest groups in the society in which he lives quickly and viciously quash any hint of real personal or social progress. The

111

best thinkers are maligned by his own in-group. Popular accounts of philosophy get "dumbed down", while professionals make names for themselves by **competing in the complexity of their theories.** Besides, the man thinks, since people are mostly alike, how could anyone be more rational than himself? Aren't science and technology the only fields of endeavor needed to solve our problems?

IF 999 PEOPLE TELL ME THAT MY BOOK FAILED,
BUT ONE TELLS ME THAT IT IS A SUCCESS,
I WILL KNOW THAT I SUCCEEDED.
The Author

THE LIMITS OF SCIENCE AND TECHNOLOGY, SCIENCE, SCIENCE-FICTION, PSEUDO-SCIENCE

TO BE SURE, WE MUST TAKE CARE NOT TO CONFUSE
THE LIMITS OF OUR PRESENT KNOWLEDGE WITH
THE LIMITS OF WHAT THERE IS TO BE KNOWN.
Hoimar Von Ditfurth
Children Of The Universe

WHY DO THINGS GO WRONG?
BECAUSE MAKING THEM GO RIGHT IS HARD.
ON THE ONE HAND ERROR IS INTOLERABLE,
WHILE ON THE OTHER MISTAKES ARE INEVITABLE.
The New Yorker, 1999
Dr. Atul Gawande
"When Doctors Make Mistakes"

THE ESSENCE OF SCIENCE IS THAT
IT IS THE OPPOSITE OF SUPERSTITION
The Author

It was pointed out that the mere acquisition of facts and knowledge is **only an aspect** of the virtue of Intellectual Curiosity – that the virtue includes, among other things, an interest in a **variety** of topics, and a certain **attitude** toward the acquisition and use of knowledge itself. It was also emphasized that none of the three Primary Virtues, if practiced alone, are in any way adequate for a man and that, indeed, it is virtually impossible to practice any without practicing them all. In this topic I wish to continue to explore what the acquisition of knowledge (science and information), and its application (technology), can, and cannot, do for man.

In the field of **pure science** there is an ultimate limit to what man will be able to know, and that limit is now being approached. In the field of the **very small,** (particle physics), scientists try to understand just exactly what is "existence" – of what is stuff made and why does it behave as it does? Here are found a bewildering number of tiny particles, each of which (presumably) fulfills a particular function to create the world we experience. Scientists have made heroic efforts in making sense of this, but no theory has yet been completely satisfactory. Even if all possible particles could be observed (and how could we be certain when all possibilities had been exhausted?), there would remain the task of making sense of it all – a daunting prospect.

In the field of the **very large,** (astrophysics), scientists study the behavior of unbelievably large quantities of material and energy at both very close, as well as incredibly large distances. As telescopes have progressed, scientists are seeing things that tax the imagination and defy explanation. Due to some kind of providence, it turned out that the **farther away** man looks with his telescopes the **farther back in time** he also sees, allowing man to explain very much indeed. A good telescope is **literally a time machine.** However, it is now known that there is a limit to this too, which appears to be something under 14 BILLION years. Beyond some limit objects appear to be moving away from us so fast that they simply disappear! In addition it appears that there is no center to the whole thing, with no particular point of observation being better than any other, and also no edge!

As I write, the "new" space telescope (JWST) will be launched tomorrow. The "old" space telescope has been in operation for nearly 30 years now. Prior to "the Hubble", astrophysicists felt that they had a fairly good handle on things. But data provided by Hubble, valuable as it is, undeniably deepened the mystery.

113

It remains to be seen whether JWST will answer more questions than it raises. One thing is for certain: according to the premise of this Book there is an explanation **for what we see,** the only question being whether man can decipher the information he has, or acquire any needed new information. That is Science.

If all these observations of our world do not boggle one's mind then one is either asleep or has lost his sense of wonder. Some additional things will eventually be explained **provisionally,** however, the bottom line is that ultimately it will come down to theories which will not be provable, since man can only prove what he can perceive and conceive!

Between the very small and the very large, man pretty much understands everything – at least in principle – except **consciousness.** No one has proposed any satisfactory theories on how a brain can achieve this "awareness", yet it is clear that it is possessed by man as well as many animals. It remains to be seen whether man will ever fully understand how the **brain** accomplishes the totality of its functions, even though its various **cells** and their **separate activities** are quite well understood. Man may never fully understand exactly how DNA is able to make a living thing in all its complexity.

> IT IS THAT UNOCCUPIED SPACE WHICH MAKES A ROOM INHABITABLE,
> AS IT IS OUR LEISURE HOURS WHICH MAKE LIFE ENDURABLE.
> Lin Yutang
> The Importance Of Living

In the field of applied science, (technology), man has passed the tipping point in his "toys", and their annoyance, as well as their danger, has surpassed their material benefits. How big does a television really need to be? Or for that matter, how many pixels? How "smart" do our TVs or homes need to be? Our TVs are now WATCHING US! Do you have a "smart home"? -- the government can change your thermostat from Washington D.C. Do I need to mention computer and soft-ware compatibility problems? Roads are constructed to closer and closer tolerances – pot holes then appear right on schedule. The equipment to coordinate traffic signals has never been better, yet the coordination of signals has never been worse, as those managing the systems are lazy or stupid or corrupt. Driving a car (you can tell from all this that I love driving) is perhaps the most pleasurable and exciting experience available to the average human, yet there are those who wish to take it away with **self-driving cars** -- for the love of Hell.! There is something wrong with a person who doesn't enjoy driving and wishes this joy away.

114

Let's talk about some more serious aspects of technology. Statists are working towards a cash-less society, which they can now engineer with technology. We love the internet and feel that it gives us power, yet it is thoroughly monitored, commercialized, censored, and will be shut down at the first sign that it is needed for organized resistance. Because of the internet the government can now know the political persuasion of almost any person prior to dealing with them, such as, **1)** grading your child's school work, **2)** granting a business license, **3)** pulling one over for a driving infraction, **4)** sending police to one's home, **5)** picking **your** jury, **6)** drawing voting districts, 7) etc., etc. Children, exhibiting addictive behavior due to their already damaged rationality, are finally destroyed by unsupervised, unmanaged access to the internet. There are more and more cameras appearing in public places – citizens have lost their anonymity. The people are giving away their **secret ballot** with technology. The government's snooping on the people, with technology, is ever increasing. The government is developing small arms that do not "pull the trigger" until the shot is guaranteed to strike the target – the people will of course be prohibited this technology. Our police have been militarized, initially in the name of the drug war, yet will be turned onto the people when needed. Did you know that there is **no practical limit** to the size of a hydrogen-fusion atomic bomb (the so-called H-bomb)?....... well now you do. But, more likely, billions of us will starve to death and/or kill each other. Our technology has facilitated, and the lack of socio-economic progress caused, the world population to mushroom out of control and the Earth cannot continue to carry this pressure much longer. Non-renewable resources are being used up at a frightening rate. I will say more on this in the next Topic.

I also wish to say a few words about science-fiction and false science. In better days writers such as Isaac Asimov wrote both "straight science" as well as science-fiction. When writing science, the reader was given the facts of science as known at the time. The distinction between science and science-fiction was at least implicitly maintained by the author, and at least to some extent by his audience. However, this is almost non-existent in today's popular culture. Today's audience wishes to be entertained with a mix of real science, science-fiction, and false science, often in the form of political agendas – with no distinction made between them! Such an approach might provide entertainment or political propaganda, but is useless for promoting science. When there is a market for something there will always be men who will come to fill that demand. So, as I write, there are any number of **popular** science personalities writing books, giving speeches, producing media programs, etc., with **none of them** doing straight science – all produce a mix of science, science-fiction, "gee-whizz", and political propaganda. I will say that, among the **current** crop of **popular** personalities which presently come to my mind, the worst is Michio Kaku. I considered mentioning some of the better **popular** science personalities, but decided that none of the **popular ones** deserve it. You can fool most of the people most of the time. I must mention, however, that on the internet I am aware of some scientists, such as Anton Petrov, for example, who are good and seem to be doing pretty much straight science -- and I encourage and commend them **to the extent that they are.** There are certainly other good ones that I am not aware of. It is these people who should be sought out and supported. A scientist is not necessarily a philosopher nor proper political scientist.

Perhaps the most popular and effective method for pushing false science is the equating of "correlation" with "causation", or the closely related trick of assuming that one knows which events are the "cause" and which are the "effects", when one may, in fact, not know at all. That two events occur in proximity is not proof that one caused the other, nor does it necessarily prove **which one** caused the other if there is indeed a connection. The current par excellence example of these is as follows: Neurologists claim the ability to map out "active areas" in the brain. A subject is then put through various tests which promote the subject to think or feel things. Then, depending upon which areas of the brain appear more active, the conclusion is made that the subjects' brain was in some way "hard wired" to think in that way – i.e., that the intense activity was the "cause" while the various thought processes and feelings were merely the "effect". My main point here is not whether such claims are true, but that ZERO effort is made by the scientific establishment to prove or provide evidence to the **general public** that such conclusions are warranted. In general, the society is looking for **non-volitional** explanations for the human condition. There is no money in free will. In fact, it is more likely that the reverse conclusion is the correct one! We have already shown that a man's thought processes and emotions are not predetermined.

THE NEAR-TERM FATES OF MANKIND

STANDING TOUGH UNDER THE STARS AND STRIPS
WE CAN TELL
THIS DREAM'S IN SIGHT
YOU'VE GOT TO ADMIT IT
AT THIS POINT IN TIME THAT IT'S CLEAR
THE FUTURE LOOKS BRIGHT

Donald Fagen
I.G.Y.

THE DEPTH OF YOUR GRIEF WILL BE THE DEPTH OF YOUR LOVE.
Joanna Macy

I am not certain whether this Topic should be presented with a nod to Donald Fagen or with apologies to him. Mr. Fagen was a fine lyricist and with a sarcastic, ironic bent, as seen in a number of his works. I say "was" a fine lyricist, even though as I write he still walks! – but hey, we have to plan ahead, right? (that one's for you Mr. Fagen.) Anyways, Fagen was likely being at least a bit sarcastic or ironic in I.G.Y., and in that spirit this topic is presented.

The concerns regard two things that will happen to man, **by his own hand,** within the next 100 to 200 years. In fact, I believe that these changes are already underway. That man will deal with these eventualities **irrationally** is a virtual certainty – causing injustice and suffering beyond description.

Before proceeding, familiarize oneself with at least the following concepts:

1) GNP -- (Gross National Product) The yearly total value of all goods and services produced or provided by every person in a society.

2) Cargoism   -- The belief in limitless resources

3) Cornucopianism -- The belief that technology will always save us.

4) Fate   -- A final outcome not intended by anyone, but resulting from innumerable small decisions about other matters, by innumerable people

C. Write Mills
Sociologist

Since man inhabits this material world he ultimately needs access to sufficient resources needed to sustain his life. Further, man then performs "value added" activities upon these resources, as well as "services" in the service industry – all these activities require "resources". Man then must decide, via. the **free market,** how to allocate his resources and human labor among his needs and wants.

One "great sorrow", I hypothesize, will concern man's **medical needs.** Modern medicine, as well as the very existence of civilization itself, saves numerous people who would otherwise have been lost due to a wide variety of natural causes. This process has been occurring for some time now. Perhaps the most stark example of this is the modern child mortality rate when compared to that of the past. Most of these survivors then grow up to have offspring of their own, thus passing on genetic traits that **may** otherwise have been taken out by pre-technology natural selection. It is thus that each passing generation needs, on average, a bit more medical care resources than its predecessor. For a long time now the medical field has been very much a growth industry. Is this growth due only to advances in treatments and patient longevity? Or can some of it be attributed to the process I describe above? It would seem that the process I describe is real and is un-doing millions of years of very careful and hard-won selection by nature.

The long term result of such a process would be an ever-increasing demand for resources, manpower in particular, by the medical field. The cost of medical care is already highly exacerbated due in large part to the massive amount of easy government money which has flowed into the system. How much of our GNP is currently spent on medical care? How much is it increasing? How much is man willing to spend? How much CAN he spend on medical care before such spending begins to impinge upon other pressing needs? It would seem that man has some grievous decisions to make in the relatively near future.

The process I describe may have at least some respect for national boundaries – with the more advanced societies experiencing **more** of the described phenomenon! Nor should it be taken that this Topic is a call for more socialized medicine, or socialized anything! – as it certainly is not. By right and by justice the costs of medical care are borne by individual men or through their private insurance companies.

WELL I THINK IT'S FINE BUILDING JUMBO PLANES
OR TAKING A RIDE ON A COSMIC TRAIN
SWITCH ON SUMMER FROM A SLOT MACHINE
YES, GET WHAT YOU WANT TO IF YOU WANT
CAUSE YOU CAN GET ANYTHING.

YES, I KNOW WE'VE COME A LONG WAY
WE'RE CHANGING DAY TO DAY
BUT TELL, ME WHERE DO THE CHILDREN PLAY?
                                    "Where Do The Children Play"
                                    Cat Stevens

The other catastrophe I call attention to, the real one, will respect no national boundaries -- it is **the final depletion of the Earth's non-renewables**.

Largely as a result of man's medical and technological progress, man asked the Earth to support, **in lavish comfort, style, and waste,** far more people than could have been comfortably accommodated indefinitely. In 1954, Harrison Brown published, <u>The Challenge Of Man's Future: An Inquiry Concerning the Conditions of Man During The Years That Lie Ahead</u>, and in 1957, a follow-up volume, <u>The Next Hundred Years</u>. These books need to be read by every thinking person. They point to **massive changes** for mankind. Although understandable, in my opinion the tone of the books is optimistic beyond warrant. They assume an heroic, almost superhuman and unimaginable level of human cooperation and integrity of world leaders and other people in power. Further, they overlook any number of details, such as the possible negative effect of loss of the "ecosystem", as the world they describe will have little room for large wild open spaces or many of the animal and plant species we now take for granted. Can the Earth really be converted into one **giant wind farm-solar panel-hydroelectric-factory-mining-farming-housing development?** We generously excuse those volumes for their optimism as they were from a better time with the average man being of higher intelligence and integrity, and the corruption of leaders better hidden. Most people just do not realize how much world population and lifestyles are dependent upon easily recoverable resources – which are coming to an end. Judging by man's past performance in ethics and politics, the expectations regarding his future behavior on this matter are truly grim.

119

Just as an aside, it is worth noting that, throughout human history, most of the value of the **extraction and sale** of natural resources has been plundered by despotic rulers and corrupt governments, (the phrase "blood diamond" doesn't come from nowhere), as opposed to any possible rightful land owners. Few societies have had even a semblance of justice on this issue – the United States being the most notable exception! The very **concept** of truly private ownership of property is itself a relatively new idea, and never yet fully achieved.

Please understand that this "wall" I describe will not be one of degree but of **kind** – it will have little to do with the then-world population. The problem will not be one of demand, but of supply! Until now, when man wanted more goods or services he simply employed more slaves, cut more wood, tilled more land, mined more ore, drilled more oil, built more dams or conquered more peoples. So this topic does not describe anything that man has dealt with previously. Further, the problems postulated are in addition to the fact that mankind **refuses to live free,** and the ominous, ever presence of nuclear weapons.

Neither of the threats postulated constitute lifeboat situations which would be exceptions to the ideas presented in this Book and justify an un-free world. As long as men have meaningful options there is no "equal right to resources" -- there are only private property rights, trade, and charity (if feasible!). There is no "right" to medical care, nor even to the last loaf of bread on Earth; for medical care is provided by other men, and a **free man** will always be able to grow at least one more loaf of bread. The bottom line is that man cannot continue indefinitely to smooth over his problems with scientific or technological discovery, and political jury-rigging. Men just do not realize that the acceptance of right ideas, **regardless of any other consideration,** is a life or death issue.

I DO NOT KNOW NOW WW 3 WILL BE FOUGHT,
BUT WW 4 WILL BE FOUGHT WITH
STICKS AND STONES

Albert Einstein

AND THE SINS OF THE FATHER SHALL BE VISITED UPON SEVEN GENERATIONS

DIFFICULT TIMES CREATE STRONG MEN
STRONG MEN CREATE EASY TIMES
EASY TIMES CREATE WEAK MEN
WEAK MEN CREATE DIFFICULT TIMES
G. Michael Hopf

The purpose of this Topic is to point out the principle that once a certain road is taken it becomes difficult for a man, or a society, to choose another road -- the father down the road is travelled, the more difficult change becomes, the greater and more in-soluble become problems, and the more obscure become their root causes.

Life presents a man with an endless series of ethical choices (recall the **full** meaning of Ethics from Part 3). If a man consistently makes rational choices his life steadily becomes more stable, even easier and natural feeling. On the other hand as a man, or a society, consistently chooses the irrational path correction becomes increasingly difficult -- problems will mount and some will eventually become insoluble by normal means, finally leading to some kind of collapse.

Most men have so much invested in their particular erroneous ways of being that no fundamental change in them is to be expected -- but such did not have to be. Life presents a man with many small choices along his way, as well as some big ones. In the many smaller choices it would be relatively easy for him to take the high road, but it is also so tempting for another man to take what seems to be the easy way out. The difference between the two men lies in their **relationship to the Primary Virtues.** The Primary Virtues are the **"irreducible primaries" of thought** and are necessary for the development of the derivative virtues. To the extent that a man is Intellectually Independent, Curious and Honest he will understand how, in all the little things of life, to take the high road and why he should do it. This will prepare the man for making the right decisions when the tougher problems in life come along.

121

The above is a partial list of topics that came to me as I wrote the Book. However, I offer the following additional thoughts for the reader to himself consider now that he has read The Handbook On Understanding:

1) How "universal" are ideas presented in this Book? Would they apply to any volitional beings anywhere in the Universe? Would intelligent beings elsewhere be "volitional"?

2) Has the Earth been visited by beings from other worlds?

3) Do we honor men for their discoveries, or is it truer to say we honor them for being "the first", i.e., for being "innovators"?

4) What actually is "intuition"?

5) What are "taboos"? Why are they so powerful?

6) What is "hazing" in all its forms?

7) Is there a best election system? Should judges be "independent", or elected?

> A MAN WHO MAKES A MISTAKE
> AND DOESN'T CORRECT IT
> HAS MADE ANOTHER MISTAKE.
>
> Confucius

122

AFTERWARD

AN OLD MAN, I READ THE BOOK OF LIFE AS QUICKLY AS A SINGLE SENTENCE IN MY CHILDHOOD.
Guy Murchie

What does a first and only time author say after he has said all that he can think to say? One of my heroes is Neil Armstrong. With what little of him that I know he was a beautiful man of the Primary Virtues. All things considered, that he was among those available, and that he came to be the first, is certainly among the most serendipitous events in the history of mankind. For the record, and equally fitting for the first man as well as ourselves, he was an **aeronautical engineer** all in training, in career, and in heart. For the rest of his life, to my knowledge, he carried the distinction with as much or more grace as anyone. In those timeless moments on the ladder, "Mr. Science" had certainly earned an intensity of emotion that we can scarcely imagine. And how could we possibly begrudge? Yet, to this day there are those who, equally driven by another kind of emotion, would walk up to the man and scream at this angel what a liar he is – that the landing never happened. Such are the extremes of human character – of which this author is far from either, but hopefully much closer to one.

"LET NONE SAY THAT THE ENGINEER IS AN UNSOCIABLE CREATURE WHO DELIGHTS ONLY IN FORMULAE AND SLIDE RULES"
Plea in MIT Yearbook
Genius: The Life And Science Of
Richard Feynman
James Gleick

When we students were finishing engineering school there was a seminar course, and I remember well two suggestions the teachers had for us. One was that "An education was what we would have left after we forgot everything we learned in school.", (a comforting thought for students who might have studied much harder than I did). In the terms of this Book, we would say that though many of the details of our study would be forgotten, the concepts we learned would remain. The non-conceptual mentality more fears the forgetting of details, since these represent a greater proportion of its knowledge than for the highly conceptual thinker. For the conceptual man the details of knowledge are of less importance – it is the concepts he really values.

123

The second suggestion was that though most of us might end up at some mundane engineering workstation, there was no reason why each of us couldn't have at least one "original good idea" during our lives. I hope that I have presented the reader with some novel and useful insights in this Book. Is this my good idea? The reader will have to judge. Even so, I didn't want my most cherished ideas to die with me at some point. So I wrote this Book.

When I finished engineering school I was young and naïve, and perhaps projecting into other people too much of my own attitudes. I was under the impression that engineers were a kind of very special breed, in that they were significantly more rational than even other professionals. The high intellectual powers of the instructors in university, as well as the apparent willingness of we students to be led by talent, had jaded me. Though engineers, due to their rational approach to mechanical things, are indeed somewhat more rational than the general population, there is room for improvement just as with anyone else. In the "real world" I found people in my profession who were just as covetous of their own positions, and just as envious of other's good ideas, as anyone else. Paraphrasing that old saw -- "Rationality is just where you find it."

I would like to share with the reader, and place in the record, a couple of additional personal stories relating to topics discussed in this Book, that are meaningful to me. I share these things in the spirit of teaching.

In the first story, I was working in a lab and had not been there very long at all. One day, some subordinates came to me with an idea which they had been trying to implement, but with no luck, as one of their co-workers, who's cooperation was needed, was blocking it – he was being an ass. I'm making an educated guess that these subordinates had never approached **my superior** with the same request because they were afraid to, assuming he would be unwilling to rock the boat by taking their side -- even though he was the boss! So I am thinking that these subordinates **saw something in me,** and approached me with their idea. I considered it for a few moments, saw nothing wrong with it, and approached "the ass" and asked him to make the paperwork change. He really blew up, but made the change and it turned out to be a great thing! In fact, the change probably even helped HIM at his work station. To this day I am honored that those guys approached me with their idea and am glad to have made a difference.

The second story is from my high school days. A class called Industrial Arts, and there are four boys at each table, mine included, (I, the only one in the class destined for engineering school). Each of us builds a model rocket of paper and cardboard. All of the rockets look the same, superficially, but each model has a different internal design. The model that each boy built had been chosen by lots, (pure chance), **and this was made obvious.** After building our rockets, the teacher tells us to vote on which airframe is the best. Each boy votes for the airframe that HE had built, as did I. I had seen something in my model which caused me to vote for it. Afterwards, the teacher told us which of the models was considered superior – it was the one I had built. To this day I regret that I built the model that I did, and would prefer to have built any of the other models to know if I would have crossed over and supported the correct model even though I had not built it.

> But surpassing all stupendous inventions, what sublimity of mind was his who dreamed of finding a means of communicating his deepest thoughts to any other person, though distant by mighty intervals of place and time! Of talking with those who are in India, of speaking to those who are not yet born and will not be born in ten thousand years – and with what facility?
> By the different arrangement of twenty characters upon a page!
> Galileo Galilei
> Dialogue Concerning The Two Chief World Systems

READING MAKETH A FULL MAN,
AND WRITING AN EXACT MAN
Francis Bacon

I am moved by the arts of reading and writing. Isn't it magnificent how a person can write down ideas, and then later on, in one year or 1000, have those exact ideas reproduced in another person's brain. Even if alien beings discovered mankind and acquired our records, they would decipher our writings and they too would experience the precise ideas encoded by the writer. A million or more years from now, should intelligent being still occupy this land, they will have evolved into a new species other than ourselves, unable to interbreed with homo sapiens – yet they will be using the knowledge that we started – an experience that we ourselves can never have.

It is reading and writing that is truly unique to man, and is a requirement for stable intellectual progress. Each word in a language, other than proper nouns, represents a concept. Recall that concepts are for "saving thinking", thereby making thinking more efficient. I think it is said that the English Language has more words in usage than any other. This may be more than coincidence – it may represent a greater attempt at conceptualization of life by the English Speaking peoples. Such, and so much more, are the wonderful things provided by reading and writing. Considering all books, both existing and that as yet to be produced, I am impressed by how many people have something valuable to say. I feel small. However, from time to time, as I'm reading a book, I will find therein a good idea of my own that I have had before. The satisfaction provided by these moments is cherished! Sad that I often let them come and go, with the particular passages, or their location, forgotten, unless I make a special point of remembering. Oh well, I'll just keep reading.

I think that old books are better than new books for at least the following reasons:

1) Old writers were, on average, more honest and wise than new writers.
2) Since history is the future unfolded, it is easier to spot a smart old writer than a smart new writer.
3) It is easier to spot a stupid old writer than a stupid new writer.
4) Old books are cheaper than new books.
5) Old books smell better than new books.

I do not like the electronic books displayed on a computer screen. I want a book I can hold and flip pages easily. It is with gladness that I have heard these horrible things are on the decline. They are "time killers" mostly, not well suited to learning. Need I mention what my feelings on the "audio books" might be? Our schools and libraries are throwing away a lot of their investment in material resources (books and such -- except for romance and action novels, movies and gaming media), and paying **middle men** royalties for access to electronic books and periodicals. This is CRIMINAL! -- I don't care what the law says.

> "The hunting-down and destruction of books had been done
> with the same thoroughness in the (common) quarters as
> anywhere else. It was very unlikely that there existed
> anywhere in (the Country) a copy of a book printed
> earlier than 1960."
>
> George Orwell
> Nineteen Eighty-Four

Have you noticed in this Book that some fundamental things have tended to come in "threes"? I attempted to come up with some grand theory to explain this, but as yet I have made no progress – perhaps the reader can come up with something. I just thought I'd mention that.

An important goal in this Book was to conceptualize the issues down to a manageable number of fundamental things to focus on. I have given you the "prime numbers" of life. But one final suggestion sums up what I hope the reader takes from the Work as a whole - **think adequately before taking strong actions or positions on anything.** The more significant the act, or the more grave its consequences, the greater the need for one to **know** one is correct. The evil is simply the irrational when given the opportunity to act. Since no one is absolutely 100% rational, we all have some potential evil within ourselves. Evil is not something "in that other guy over there". The numbers of truly evil men in the world only partly accounts for the way things are. It is the "useful idiots" who give their support to evil people that really run the world. Evil people tend to be clever, if not intelligent. The person of average intelligence and rationality is no match for the evil manipulators who tend to seek positions of power and prestige. So stop giving one's support to clever but evil people. Nothing bad will happen just because one doesn't get his $0.02 in on every issue. In fact things will improve – I guarantee it. There are a few very smart people who do have everyone's best interest at heart. Find these people and support them, listen, and learn – or at least get out of their way.

I end my work as I began it, by being honest and forthcoming with the reader. If the existence of the United States and its Constitution was not a bright enough light to end the darkness in the World, once and for all, then what would be? **Only if enough people became much better thinkers.** I offer as the final quote, my final message:

WHAT IS THE VALUE OF A HUMAN LIFE?
HOW SHOULD YOU TRY TO LIVE YOUR LIFE?

I SUGGEST THAT THE ANSWERS ARE TO
BE FOUND AS IF MAN DISCOVERED THAT
EVERY HUMAN JOY OR SUFFERING,
EVERY HUMAN SUCCESS OR FAILURE,
EVERY HUMAN GOOD DEED OR EVIL,
AND ALL OF OUR LOVE,
ECHOED ACROSS THE UNIVERSE FOR ETERNITY

INVITATION

There is so much that I have not said in the writing of this Book. There are several books I own which I have read more than once due to their great value, and a number of others I plan to read again for their value and for pleasure,,,,,,, time permitting. If you found value in this Book I encourage you to read it again; I promise you that you will benefit from that.

I invite you to correspond with me. If you found value in this book, or did not, I would like to hear of your experiences. If you did find value in this book, then share it.

Now go.

rodney203@aol.com

RESOURCES AND EXAMPLE READING LIST

**EVERYTHING THAT NEEDS TO BE SAID
HAS ALREADY BEEN SAID;
BUT SINCE NOBODY WAS LISTENING,
EVERYTHING MUST BE SAID AGAIN.**
Andre' Gide

No book should be a dead end. A good book points the reader to other interesting books and areas of inquiry. Therefore, in the spirit of Intellectual Curiosity the following list is offered. The listing is in addition to uncounted other books, articles, essays, speeches and conversations experienced by the author.

Note: The reference to any thinker in this Book is not to be construed to mean that the author agrees with all of that thinker's conclusions or behavior.

==

A LECTURE SERIES

The V-50 Lectures   The "V" stands for "volition"
An extensive series of excellent lectures delivered by a man named Jay Snelson, as the senior lecturer at the now defunct Free Enterprise Inst. The message of the lectures is <u>mildly</u> anarchistic, but they are highly recommended. Lecture segments may be found on youtube. They were originally published as a boxed set of CDs. If you can find a used set you will probably pay $$ for it. It appears that no one is selling quantities of them now. A book transcription of the lectures was published, called "Sic Itur Ad Astra" (This Is The Way To The Stars). Good luck finding a copy of that as well.

A TEXTBOOK SERIES

Current Thinking And Writing, First Series   1946 | I discovered this series of
Current Thinking And Writing, Second Series 1951 | texts at a flea market. They
Current Thinking And Writing, Third Series   1956 | were intended for freshman
Current Thinking And Writing, | college level English courses
Current Thinking And Writing, Fifth Series   1964 | during better days of
Current Thinking And Writing, Sixth Series   1969 | education. I am enjoying
reading them. I have been
unable to find the 4th series.

PHILOSOPHY ("Hard" and "Soft")
- Books on Objectivism   There are many various
                                                 books by Ayn Rand and
                                                 her associates that can be
                                                 easily found

- Objectivism: The Philosophy Of Ayn Rand   1991 Leonard Peikoff
- Return To Reason   1971 Paul Lepanto
                                                  A primer on Objectivism
- The Ayn Rand Companion   1984 Mimi Gladstein
- Three bound collections of Objectivist newsletters
    a) The Objectivist Newsletter
    b) The Objectivist
    c) The Ayn Rand Letter
- Judgement Day: My Years With Ayn Rand   1989 Auto-bio by N. Branden
- The Passion Of Ayn Rand   1986 Bio by Barbara Branden
- The Philosophic Thought Of Ayn Rand   1984 Den Uyl/Rasmussen
- Ayn Rand And The World She Made   2009 Anne Heller
- Goddess Of The Market   2009 Jennifer Burns
- The Letters Of Ayn Rand   1995 Rand's correspondence
- Discovery Of Freedom   1943 Rose Wilder Lane
                                                  (and she finished high
                                                  school in Crowley
                                                  Louisiana!)

- The God Of The Machine   1943 Isabel Paterson's famous
                                                  book
- A Guide For The Perplexed   1977 E.F. Schumaker
- Computer Power And Human Reason   1976 J. Weizenbaum
- An Introduction To The Objectivist Comm. ,,,, 2001 James Yoke
- The Writings Of Kahlil Gibran
- This I Believe   1997 E.F. Schumacher
- Actual Ethics   2006 James Otteson
- Lost In Thought: The Hidden Pleasures Of ,,,, 2020 Zena Hitz

POLITICAL PHILOSOPHY
- The Conscience Of A Conservative   1960 Barry Goldwater
                                                  (actually L. Brent Bozell Jr.)
- Common Sense   1776 Thomas Paine
- All The Shah's Men   2003 Stephen Kinzer
- Overthrow   2006 Stephen Kinzer
- Theft Of A Nation   1982 William W. Baker
- Goliath: Life And Loathing In Greater Israel 2013 Max Blumenthal

Cont.--
- Through Our Enemies Eyes	2006	Michael Scheuer
- Imperial Hubris	2004	Michael Scheuer
- The Coming Anarchy	2000	Robert D. Kaplan
- An Empire Wilderness	1998	Robert D. Kaplan
- The Arabists	1993	Robert D. Kaplan
- John Marshall And The Constitution	1919	Corwin
- A Nation Of Sheep	1961	William Lederer
- Somebody's Gotta Say It	2007	Neil Boortz
- The Federalist Papers	1787	Hamilton, Madison, Jay
- The Road To Serfdom	1944	Friedrich Hayek
- Your Disobedient Servant	1978	Chapman (book from U.K.)
- Arguably	2012	Christopher Hitchens (essays)
- The Gulag Archipelago		Aleksandr I. Solzhenitsyn
- In Defense Of Freedom	1996	Frank Meyer
- Generation Of Vipers	1943	Philip Wylie
- The Magic Animal	1968	Philip Wylie
- The Proper Study Of Mankind	1948	Stuart Chase

SELF HELP / SOCIAL IMPROVEMENT

- Curse Of The High I.Q.	2016	Aaron Clarey
- Enjoy The Decline	2013	Aaron Clarey
- The Manipulated Man	1971	Esther Vilar
- The Polygamous Sex	1974	Esther Vilar (a rare book)
- The Rational Male	2013	Rollo Tomassi
- The Woman Racket	2008	Steve Moxon (from U.K.)
- Games People Play	1964	Eric Berne
- Lets Really Make Love	1995	Robert Rimmer
- Listening To The Littlest	1984	Ruth Reardon
- Life 101	1991	Rodger / McWilliams
- Cultural Literacy: What Every American,,,,,,,	1988	E.D. Hirsch, Jr.
- The Mature Mind	1949	H.A. Overstreet
- The Road Less Travelled	1978	M. Scott Peck
- The Hearts Of Men	1983	Barbara Ehrenreich
- Understanding Human Nature	1927	Alfred Adler
- Basic Writings In The History Of Psy.	1979	Robert Watson
- Some Books By Dr. Ron Smothermon		

SCIENCE
- Books about Richard P. Feynman

There are numerous books about Feynman that have been written by his friends and admirers

- Galileo's Commandment: 2500 Years Of Great   1997 Edmund Bolles
- Historical Geology (textbook)   2000 Wicander/Monroe
- The Making Of The Atomic Bomb   1986 Richard Rhodes
    (see Rhodes' auto-bio below)

- Dark Sun   1995 Richard Rhodes
    (making the hydrogen bomb)

- The Sidereal Messenger   Galileo's notebook
- Seeing And Believing   1998 Richard Panek
- From Copernicus To Einstein   1942 Hans Reichenbach
- The Scientific Companion, 2nd ed. (textbook)   1995 Cesare Emiliani
- Universe In Focus   1997 Stuart Clark
    (story of the Hubble Telescope

- The Roving Mind   1997 Isaac Asimov
- Asimov On Physics   1976 Isaac Asimov
- One, Two, Three, Infinity   1947 George Gamow
- The Philosophy Of Physical Science   1939 Arthur Eddington
- The Challenge Of Man's Future   1954 Harrison Brown
- The Next Hundred Years   1957 Brown/Bonner/Weir
- Beyond Oil   2005 K. Deffeyes
- Rust   2015 Jonathan Waldman
- Thirty Years That Shook Physics   1966 George Gamow
- Quantum: Einstein, Bohr And The Great,,,,,,   2008 M. Kumar
- On The Revolutions Of Heavenly Spheres   Nicholas Copernicus
- Children Of The Universe   1970 Hoimar Von Ditfurth
- The Story Of Science   1931 David Dietz
- Dialogue Concerning The Two Chief World Systems   Galileo Galilei

GEOGRAPHY
- The Fourth Part Of The World   2009 Toby Lester
    (story of the lost map of America)

- Isaac's Storm   1999 Erik Larson
    (the 1900 Galveston Hurricane)

Cont.
- Alaska's Wilderness Highway   1994 Mike Jensen
                                                             (traveling the Dalton Road)
- The Last Two Million Years   1973 Readers Digest
- Atlas Of The Prehistoric World   1999 Douglas Palmer
- The Story Of Maps   1949 Lloyd Brown
- The Historical Atlas Of The Earth (textbook)   1996 Osborne/Tarling
- Historical Geology (textbook)   2000 R Wicander/J. Monroe

SCIENCE BIOGRAPHY
- Books on Richard Feynman
- First Man   2005 James Hansen
                                                             (bio of Neil Armstrong)
- American Prometheus   2005 Bird/Sherwin
                                                             (bio of Robert Oppenheimer)
- Einstein   1971 Ronald Clark
- Slide Rule   1954 Nevil Shute
                                                             (airships and early airplanes)
- The Last Man Who Knew Everything   2005 Andrew Robinson
                                                             (bio of Thomas Young)
- Return To Earth   1973 Buzz Aldrin/Warga
- Deke! U.S. Manned Space From Mercury,,,,,,,,,   1995 Deke Slayton/M. Cassutt
- At The Edge Of Space: The X-15 Flight Prog.   1992 Milton O. Thompson
- The Human Side Of Science   2016 Wiggins/Wynn
- Scientific Autobiography And Other Papers   1949 Max Planck
- The Voyage Of The H.M.S. Beagle   1839 Charles Darwin

GENERAL BIOGRAPHY
- The Autobiography Of Benjamin Franklin
- Narrative Of The Life Of Frederick Douglass
- Incidents In The Life Of A Slave Girl   Harriet Jacobs
- An Intimate Life: Sex, Love, and My Journey,,,   2012 Cheryl Cohen-Greene
- The Description Of The World   2017 Marco Polo
                                                             (translation by Sharon
                                                             Kinoshita
- Making Love   1992 Richard Rhodes
- Undaunted Courage   1996 Stephen Ambrose
                                                             (the Lewis and Clark
                                                             expedition)
- Whips And Kisses   1991 Robert Rimmer/
                                                             C. Tavel

Cont.
- Mayflower Madam   1986 Sidney Barrows/
                                                           W. Novak

- The Importance Of Living   1937 Lin Yutang
- Ten Days: Benjamin Franklin   2008 David Colbert
                                                           (about Benjamin
                                                           Franklin)
- Over The Edge Of The World   2003 Laurence Bergreen
                                                           (Magellan's
                                                           circumnavigation)
- Song Of The Sky   1954 Guy Murchie
                                                           Aviation

SOME OUTSTANDING MOVIES

Once Upon A Time In The West	1968	To Kill A Mockingbird	1962
Lawrence Of Arabia	1968	A River Runs Through It	1992
The Good, The Bad, And The Ugly	1966	Doctor Zhivago	1965
Enemy At The Gates	2001	Planet Of The Apes	1968
The Last Emperor	1987	Empire Of The Sun	1987
The Paper Chase	1973	The Cider House Rules	1999
Jeremiah Johnson	1972	The Bridge On The River Kwai	1957
The Bridges Of Madison County	1995	Jackie Brown	1997
The Winslow Boy	1999	The Red Violin	1998
The Razors Edge	1984	Pride & Prejudice	2005
Dangerous Beauty	1998	The Remains Of The Day	1993
The Natural	1984	The Day The Earth Stood Still	1951
The Lives Of Others	2006	The Imitation Game	2014
Less Than Zero	1987	Moby Dick	1956
Seabiscuit	2003	Contact	1997
The Right Stuff	1983	The Rocky Horror Picture Show	1975
Amadeus	1984	About Time	2013
The Sessions	2012	Une Liaison Pornographique	1999
Out Of Africa	1985	Traffic	2000
Still Breathing	1997	Sicario	2015

MOVIES WORTH A LOOK

The Butler	2013	The Perez Family	1995
The Joneses	2009	Away From Her	2006
A Good Year	2006	City Island	2009
Secretary	2002	Infinity	1996
About A Boy	2002	Love Actually	2003
The Grifters	1990	Mystic River	2003
The Pledge	2001	Heaven Can Wait	1978
Trouble With The Curve	2012	The Age Of Adeline	2015

Made in the USA
Middletown, DE
19 May 2024

54552618R00091